¿Only English?

¿Only English?

**Law and Language Policy
in the United States**

Bill Piatt

University of New Mexico Press
Albuquerque

Library of Congress Cataloging-in-Publication Data

Piatt, Bill.
  ¿Only English?: law and language policy in the United
States / Bill Piatt.—1st ed.
      p.   cm.
  Includes bibliographical references.
  ISBN 0-8263-1153-9
  1. United States—Languages—Law and legislation.
2. Language policy—United States.
3. English language—Political aspects—United States.
I. Title.
KF4767.P53 1990
344.73'09—dc20
[347.3049]   89-24968

Dedicado a Rosanne, Seana, Bob y Alicia

Contents

Preface

A debate is simmering over the nation's language policy. The issue is not new. From time to time since the founding of the country numerous discussions, legal proposals, and judicial cases have centered on whether languages other than English should be recognized or even permitted here.

At the heart of the current debate are new proposals to make English the official language. A growing minority of states now have such provisions in their statutes. Several have rejected the proposal, and the matter is pending in several others. The ultimate goal of the proponents of such measures is the enactment of an amendment to the Constitution of the United States that would declare English to be the official language of this country.

Most participants in the current debate, proponents and opponents alike, are willing to view the issue as simply whether English should be the official language. Such a simplistic approach fails to take into account the important historical, legal, political and philosophical interests involved. It inevitably leads to accusations of disloyalty against those who have reservations about the proposal, and the countercharge of racism against advocates of the amendment. Lost in the name calling is any substantive analysis.

For the reasons to follow in this book, the interests at stake appear much too complex to be adequately addressed by a simple discussion of whether English (or any other language, for that matter) should be the country's official tongue. Rather, in the attempt to formulate language policy, the issues should be seen as: (1) To what extent and for what reasons do we now have the right to express ourselves and receive communications in languages other than English?; (2) How can we accommodate legitimate language interests and still maintain national cohesiveness?

We will begin this analysis in Chapter 1 with a historical perspective. Despite the efforts of many during the colonial and early national periods to establish English as the official language and create an academy to formulate language policies, the United States opted not to follow that course. Language concerns were raised again with successive waves of immigration during the middle and late 1800s. World War I brought new efforts to limit other languages. The increase in Latin American immigration following World War II and continuing up to the present, with a resulting increase in the level of bilingualism in this country, appears to be at the heart of the current debate. Chapter 1 examines why this time the language issue will not disappear with the assimilation of the language minority group, as has occurred in the past.

With a historical background, we will turn to an examination of the extent of the current legal recognition of a right to language. Constitutional provisions, case decisions, and state, federal, and local laws address the issue in an often inconsistent fashion. Nonetheless, we examine the scope of language rights in the context of the classroom (Chapter 2), the workplace (Chapter 3), the courtroom (Chapter 4), and before social service agencies (Chapter 5). Broadcasting (Chapter 6) and other areas (Chapter 7) are also addressed.

However, the development of the law in these areas has

not been consistent. Perhaps as a reflection of societal ambivalence, contradictory lines of authority have made the identification and assertion of language rights an illusive venture. It is as though the threads of language rights have not been woven into the fabric of the law, but rather surface as bothersome loose ends to be plucked off when inconvenient. Chapter 8 examines the inconsistencies and the current willingness to engage in further plucking.

Chapter 9 is a form of retreat. It asks us to regroup, given the inconsistencies, and attempt to lay a basis for an understanding of why we should recognize language rights. It considers sociological and political concerns. We are asked to consider whether the American experiment with freedom and democracy, and our geographical and economic concerns, should lead us down a different path in language issues than other countries.

Through Chapter 9 we will essentially be focusing on the first prong of the two-part analysis suggested as the better approach to the language rights issue. In Chapter 10 we address the second question: How can we accommodate legitimate language interests and still maintain national cohesiveness?

Perhaps a personal observation is appropriate before proceeding. Demographic considerations have focused the current debate on the use of the Spanish language. I consider it my good fortune both to have been born and raised in the Southwest, and to have had the opportunity to learn Spanish as well as English from family, friends, and the educational system. The town (Santa Fe) where I was born and street (Callecita) where I was raised carry Spanish names. This personal experience will inevitably be reflected in the analysis to follow. For example, it makes it difficult for me to consider Spanish a foreign language. It makes it difficult for me to see the ability to communicate in more than one language as a disadvantage.

On the other hand, the English-only movement fears that without legislative enactments, our country will eventually become almost completely bilingual. Governmental matters would be conducted in English and Spanish. Political figures and private industry alike would use languages other than English to persuade allegiance to their particular causes. People would live, love, learn, work, and play in a multilingual, multicultural atmosphere. If the scenario this movement fears should come to pass, from my perspective at least, the rest of the country would then be able to share the lifestyle and culture which I was fortunate to have experienced as a child in northern New Mexico—not a bad cultural exposure indeed.

Having now shared this perspective (bias?) with the reader, it is my hope that the following work represents an approach that avoids the simplistic, accusatory nature of the current debate, and instead could lead to the formulation of a language policy more equitably addressing legitimate concerns.

Part One

The Recurring Language Rights Debate

Chapter 1

Historical Perspective

The United States has never had an official language. The peoples in the territories that now constitute this nation have never been monolingual. However, various attempts to limit the usage of languages other than English have surfaced throughout our history. It is against this setting, and perhaps in large part due to it, that inconsistencies in the legal recognition of language rights have developed. A complete discussion of the history of language usage in this nation would require volumes. Nonetheless, some historical perspective is essential to an understanding of the contemporary law and language dilemma. In this chapter we trace the origins of our multilingualism and our tradition of official linguistic neutrality. We consider recurrent resentment by some English speakers of the presence of other languages and their speakers in our midst.

Native Tongues

English is clearly not the first language, nor even the first European language, spoken in what is now the United States of America. Prior to the beginning of the European exploration of these territories, it has been estimated that perhaps one million natives inhabited the region north of present-day Mexico and south of the polar regions. These peoples, whose ancestors immigrated from Asia across the Bering Strait, spoke up to a thousand distinct dialects and languages. Sparse settlement patterns and relatively little intertribal mingling resulted in little intercommunication. As a result, even though several language families can be identified, there was no single Indian language. One factor which may have hindered the native tongues from evolving into a few standardized languages is the apparent lack of written communications. Apparently no native language had been reduced to a formal written system by the beginning of the sixteenth century.

Policies of European colonists and succeeding American administrations, some of which can only be considered genocidal, often resulted in the extermination of the native peoples and languages. We are all too familiar with the long saga of oppression and brutalization resulting in the herding of native Americans onto isolated reservations. This herding, and the subsequent attempts to force native children into an English-speaking educational system and environment, sought to achieve the so-called civilization of these peoples including the replacement of their native tongues with English. (In the case of the conquistadores and their accompanying religious figures, the civilizing language was Spanish.)

Not all colonists, of course, supported the suppression of the natives and the stripping of their mother tongues. For example, William Penn once wrote of the Delaware language:

> I have made it my business to understand (the Delaware language) that I might not want an interpreter on any occasion. And I must say, that I know not of a language spoken in Europe that has words of more sweetness and accent or emphasis than theirs. (Conklin, p. 198)

Ironically, the herding of natives onto reservations may have been an important factor in maintenance of their languages. The learning of English on these reservations, particularly for the elderly, became unnecessary. Those who were not forcibly exposed to the educational system found little need to learn English. Navajo, Cherokee, Fox, Iroquois, and other tongues were handed down. Writing systems developed.

Instruction in native languages and renewed pride in Native American ethnicity during and following World War II served to maintain the survival of some of these tongues. As late as 1970 it was estimated that up to 300 different languages were still in use, with Navajo, Sioux, Algonquin, Pueblo, Muskhogean, and Iroquois being among the major ones. Many of these languages are spoken by only small numbers. However, more than one-third of the 800,000 native Americans in the United States in 1980 reported that they spoke an American Indian or Alaska native language. Navajo, with up to 120,000 speakers, is the largest native language in existence on our continent. It was used for transmitting military communications by the United States in the pacific theater during World War II. The Japanese were unable to break this code spoken by Navajo code talkers.

Another indigenous tongue, Hawaiian, still survives on the islands, spoken by up to 7,500 people. It remains, along with English, an official language of Hawaii.

European Arrivals

The first European language heard by the native population on this continent was Spanish. Juan Ponce de León arrived in what is now Florida in 1513, although a permanent Spanish colony was not established in that area until the founding of St. Augustine in 1565. Meanwhile, Cuba had been colonized under the Spaniard Diego Velasquez in 1511. Eight years later, an expedition led by Hernan Cortés left Cuba for the area which is now Mexico. A brutal military campaign resulted in the conquering of the natives, and the establishment of Spanish colonial rule in Mexico.

From that base, in turn, other Spanish conquistadores explored northward into what is now the American Southwest. Francisco Vásquez de Coronado traveled north, and as far east as present day Kansas, before returning to Mexico. Juan de Oñate established what has survived as the oldest continuous European settlement in the Southwest at Gabriel de los Españoles in 1598. (The area is now near the town of Española, in northern New Mexico.) Santa Fe was founded in 1609. Other settlements soon followed in what is now Colorado, Arizona, and Texas. Spain established these settlements with the religious and political goals of spreading the Spanish empire, its tongue and culture, and the Catholic religion.

In the eighteenth century, Spain pressed eastward to contain French settlements in Louisiana, and settled in California as a result of English and Russian interests in colonizing the region. The continuing presence of the Spanish language in this country is, in part, the result of this Hispanic presence representing the oldest colonial power on this continent.

The Spaniards were obviously not the only European colonizers. French traders and explorers arrived and settled in the northeastern part of the continent, as well as in the Louisiana territory. Samuel deChamplain arrived in Nova Scotia in 1604 and founded Quebec in 1608. French traders brought their language to the Great Lakes region, then down the Ohio and Mississippi rivers to Louisiana in 1682. French Huguenots settled in Charleston and New England communities in the 1680s. Although formal French political influence in the eastern colonies terminated with the French and Indian War in 1763, and in the West with the Louisiana Purchase of 1803, French language and culture have left a lasting imprint. In 1980, approximately 1.6 million Americans identified themselves as coming from homes where French was spoken. A Louisiana law still requires the teaching of the French language and the culture and history of French populations in its public schools. Proximity to French-speaking Canada has also helped to maintain the language among many Franco-Americans whose ancestors moved into New England to work in the mills and factories in the nineteenth and twentieth century. The arrival of Haitian immigrants in the last few years has provided a new source of French Creole-speaking inhabitants.

Other European languages arrived with colonizers. The Dutch established a New Netherland colony along the Hudson River in 1624. Even though the English seized control of the colony forty years later, the Dutch language continued to play an important role in the area as a second language.

Germans began arriving in Pennsylvania in 1683 and constituted one-third of the population of that region at the beginning of the revolution. Their language and culture worked to an important advantage: German-speaking colonists persuaded at least 5,000 Hessian mercenaries to defect from the British. This contribution had obviously not been foreseen by Benjamin Franklin who, in 1751, wrote:

> Why should the Palatine Boors (Germans) be suffered to swarm into our settlements and, by herding together, establish their language and matters, to the exclusion of ours? Why should Pennsylvania, founded by the English, become a colony of aliens, who will shortly be so numerous as to Germanize us instead of our Anglifying them? (Conklin, p. 69)

Anti-German sentiment resurfaced in response to the political events leading to World Wars I and II, as will be discussed later. Nonetheless, approximately 1.6 million people still speak some German in this country today. In addition, pockets of Portuguese (Massachusetts) and Swedish (New York, Minnesota, Delaware) also briefly flourished.

Clearly the most important tongue introduced by European colonizers was the English language. While the ultimate roots of English, like every other tongue, lie deep in the past, the history of the language is generally dated from approximately A.D. 1430. During this period, people known as Anglo-Saxons began immigrating into Britain. English colonists in turn introduced the language with the settlement at Jamestown in 1607. The overwhelming majority of new arrivals to the newly founded colonies were English-speaking. By the end of the century, the English-speaking areas were united as a continuous territory. However, England's policymakers chose not to designate official status for the language in its colonies.

Most English-speaking settlers arrived to pursue religious or commercial interests of their own determination. They did not arrive with the overt goal of imposing religion, language, or a political system upon the native population. Thus they did not bring either the institutional sponsorship prominent among French and Castilian colonizers. As a result, through the colonial period, although English speakers consolidated political control, and although occasionally calls were made for the recognition of English as the official language, no formal language policies or programs developed. No official language was designated nor was an official attempt made to impose linguistic standards upon new arrivals or upon the indigenous population.

Revolution and Official Linguistic Neutrality

American revolutionary leaders recognized the importance of multilingual communication to the struggle for independence from Great Britain. Their ability to spread information in languages other than English to the diverse language groups succeeded in promoting loyalty to the cause of independence. The Continental Congress, for example, published extracts from Votes and Proceedings of the Congress (1774), the Declaration of Articles Setting Forth Causes of Taking Up Arms (1775), and Resolves of Congress (1776), together with other documents, in German as well as in English. The Articles of Confederation (1777) and other documents were printed in French as well as English. The diffusion of official communications in languages other than English was seen as an important step in promoting loyalty to the new nation. The strategy succeeded. Soldiers speaking German, French, Swedish, and other languages stood with English-speaking revolutionaries in the creation of a nation committed to the liberty and independence of its peoples.

After formation of the new country, national leaders continued to look upon the maintenance of a linguistically diverse population as an asset. Many, such as Thomas Jefferson, encouraged not only the maintenance of other languages, but also the learning of foreign languages by English speakers. Another member of the Continental Congress and signer of the Declaration of Independence, Benjamin Rush, urged the teaching of German and French in American schools. He also urged the creation of a German college among Pennsylvania's citizens. He viewed such a college as the "only possible means, consistent with their liberty of spreading a knowledge of the English language among them." (Heath, p. 15).

At the same time, a view did exist that some type of standard English might be necessary in the United States. In the European monarchies, notably France and Spain, language academies existed to codify the language and prepare official dictionaries, grammars, and literary works. In 1790, John Adams proposed to the Continental Congress the creation of a "public institution for refining, correcting, improving, and ascertaining the English language" (Heath, p. 18). However, Adams was unable to persuade the Continental Congress of the need for the creation of a language academy. His proposal was killed in the committee to which it was referred.

Consistent with the early philosophy that language should not be a matter of official regulation, no law emerged during the early years of the republic designating or regulating language. Private efforts, notably by Noah

Webster, did create a type of language authority in the form of an American dictionary. Webster himself felt that no official authority should exist in language matters, and set out to create a private standard for the use of English in America. Nonetheless, when he approached Chief Justice John Marshall of the United States Supreme Court seeking endorsement of his dictionary, Marshall refused. The chief justice reminded Webster that in America individuals and not public bodies made decisions regarding language use.

Another private attempt to regulate language was the creation of the American Academy of Language and Belles Lettres in 1820. The group consisted primarily of political leaders who recognized the objections to a governmentally sanctioned language academy or policy. The academy proposed to purify and maintain a standard of writing and pronunciation. Although the group included many prestigious Americans including John Adams, Thomas Jefferson, James Madison, and James Monroe, as well as college presidents, congressmen, governors, and judicial officers, the group failed to persuade scholars, Congress, or the American people of the need for such an institution. After publishing three circulars, and receiving a good deal of criticism from, among others, Justice Marshall, the academy ceased to function, yielding to the political reality that America's early leaders had rejected national institutions whose purpose would be to limit language choice.

One scholar has summarized the relationship between law and language during the formative years of this country:

> Language choice was considered an individual matter, as were the direction and advancement of literature. Individuals were free to choose guidance through available written authorities or alliance with particular societies, which directed standardization in language according to their special interests: literary, scientific, religious, or business. What Michael Kammen has termed the 'collective individualism' (1973:116) in the culture of America's colonial period prevailed in language in the early national period as well. The

American ambiguity about whether limits upon government derived from the written text of constitutions or from an antecedent body of unwritten natural law applied also to language. Americans sought authorities, some in an academy, others in written sources or public models; yet others felt too that language was somehow natural, in the Rousseauian sense, and was governed by its own internal rules. A national language academy had proved too monarchical, too rigid for national citizens whose colonial experiences had convinced them that language and other cultural items should not be matters of national dictate. (Heath, pp. 35, 36)

Annexation and Expansion

A great many speakers of languages other than English were incorporated into the American union during its expansion. Not all of them were given a choice in the matter, and despite official language neutrality, political and racial concerns often meant their languages were not welcome.

In 1800 Spain yielded the Louisiana Territory to the French, who in turn sold it to the United States in 1803. Spain ceded Florida to the United States in 1821. Mexico, which won its independence from Spain in a revolution commencing in 1810, yielded vast portions of its territory in what is now the American Southwest following military struggles with Texas (1836) and the United States (1848). With these acquisitions, and with the Gadsden Purchase from Mexico in 1854, the United States effectively ended three hundred years of Spanish and Mexican rule over territory which now constitutes more than one-half of the land area of the contiguous forty-eight states.

Termination of political control by the French, Spanish and Mexicans did not mean an automatic and immediate assimilation of the English tongue by all of the inhabitants of these regions. Many people in what is now New Mexico, in particular, clung to the Spanish language and culture. This infuriated national commentators who repeatedly and successfully urged opposition to granting statehood to a population "who haven't troubled to learn English." New Mexico's population was characterized by one writer as "half-breeds, greasers, outlaws, etc., . . . no more fit to support a proper state government than . . . to turn missionaries." Another asked whether it would be fair to place "the mixed and half-civilized people of New Mexico on a par with the people of Massachusetts and Wisconsin" (Beck, p. 231). Statehood eventually came for New Mexico in 1912. Its constitution still guarantees the publication of laws and proposed constitutional amendments in English and Spanish. It requires teachers to be bilingual, although this has been interpreted to mean teachers must only have the opportunity to learn Spanish. Once again, the foreign language ability of its citizens served the military interests of the United States: Spanish-speaking New Mexicans (and Arizonans) formed the core of Theodore Roosevelt's Rough Riders during the Spanish-American War. Later, in World War II, New Mexican troops assigned, because of their language abilities, to the Philippines, served with distinction, even through the submission of many of them to the infamous Bataan Death March.

While at least some of the Spanish- and French-speaking inhabitants of the Southwest were brought involuntarily into the Union, virtually all of the speakers of Minde, Ewe, Ibo, Wolof, and other West African languages involuntarily arrived in the United States through the nineteenth century on slave ships. Their languages came under particular attack. Slave traders and owners prohibited slaves from communicating in native languages, acting under the fear that such private communication would help foster rebellion. At the same time, formal education was denied most slaves. As a result, slaves developed Creole languages, combining features of West African tongues with English in the colonial regions, and with French in Louisiana. Segregation patterns continued to impede complete linguistic assimilation among many American blacks. Some studies note the emergence and validity of a contemporary black English unlikely to fade from the American scene.

Immigration

Language laws, sentiments, and policies have been inextricably bound to immigration patterns and laws since colonial times. As has been seen, despite reservations by Franklin and others, non–English-speaking arrivals to the colonies found general acceptance, although occasional attacks were heard by people who questioned whether non–English-speakers would ever assimilate. However, as noted in the 1981 staff report of the Select Commission on Immigration and Refugee Policy (SCIRP—much of the material in this section was gleaned from that report), the assimilation or loyalty of new arrivals would become a familiar and often bitterly contested issue. At least in colonial times, it was not of sufficient importance to cause an official limitation upon language usage nor did it result in restrictions imposed by the colonies upon the people who would be permitted to settle in what would become the United States. In fact, one of the causes of the American Revolution as cited in the Declaration of Independence is that King George III interfered with immigration to the colonies.

After the revolution, America continued to encourage immigration. The now-familiar refrain "Give me your poor, your huddled masses yearning to breathe free" had literal significance even though the statue carrying the inscription would not be erected for some time to come, because Americans generally perceived their new nation to be a refuge for freedom-seeking peoples. Also, the sparse population (somewhat over 3 million as of the first census in 1790) indicated that a larger labor pool would be needed to build the new republic and avoid future foreign domination. While a few laws were enacted in the late 1700s and 1800s requiring residency and renunciation of allegiance to foreign powers and nobility, there were generally few restrictions imposed on immigration. One exception was the Alien Enemies Act giving the president powers to deport an alien whom the president considered dangerous to the welfare of the nation. Early state attempts to impose limits upon immigration were declared unconstitutional by the U.S. Supreme Court as violating the exclusive power of the federal government to regulate foreign commerce.

Immigrants flocked to the new United States. During the first 40 years following the end of the Revolutionary War, it is estimated that approximately 250,000 people immigrated. During the next 40 years, however, concluding with the 1860s, more than 4.5 million European immigrants arrived in the United States. At first the new immigrants were welcomed. As the numbers of immigrants began to increase dramatically by the 1840s, however, many citizens of the United States, virtually all of whom were immigrants or descendants of immigrants, began to have second thoughts. Waves of Irish immigrants entered the country during the potato famines. German-Catholic immigrants arrived following the European depressions of the 1840s. These Catholic immigrants found themselves in a country that was overwhelmingly Protestant and unofficially yet overtly hostile to Catholicism. Societies sprung up seeking to preserve the nation's ethnic purity. The Secret Order of the Star Spangled Banner and the Know Nothing Party grew out of concern, as sounded by one Protestant magazine, that "the floodgates of intemperance, pauperism and crime are thrown open by immigrants and if nothing be done to close them they will carry us back to all of the drunkenness and evil of former times" (*American Protestant Magazine*, Feb. 1849, cited in SCIRP p. 174). Violent nativism directed against the new immigrants produced bitter anti-Catholic rioting in New York, Philadelphia and Boston.

Despite the resentment surfacing against the new arrivals, immigration continued. As the country moved westward, more laborers were required to settle the frontier and lay railroads, work mines, and create an economic base. Approximately two-and-a-half million Europeans immigrated to the United States in the 1860s, and another two-and-a-half million arrived in the 1870s. During the 1880s, however, more than five million immigrants reached the American shores. Not only was there a change in the number of immigrants, but there was now a new pattern developing in European immigration. Before the 1880s, the overwhelming majority of new arrivals came from northern and western Europe. During the next two decades, approximately 70 percent of European immigrants arrived from eastern or southern Europe. Many of the Irish and German immigrants had by this time assimilated, and appeared less foreign than the new arrivals. Furthermore, even the hated Irish Catholics spoke English upon arrival. Old immigrants began to appear familiar and respectable while members of the new groups faced concerns about their inherent fitness to join the Union. Scholars began to conclude that supposed biological and cultural inferiorities, including linguistic differences, would preclude representatives of various nationalities or religious groups from ever being able to become what was called 100 percent Americans. These new immigrants were characterized, for example, by Edward Ross, a prominent academician and nativist, as "beaten men from beaten races representing the worst failures in the struggle for existence" (Joselit, cited in SCIRP, p. 179). The Yiddish, Italian, Serbo-Croation and other tongues they brought with them confirmed their inability to assimilate in the eyes of nativists.

Nonetheless, despite the growing private reservations being expressed against European immigration, the first restrictionist immigration law was not aimed at Europeans but rather at the Chinese. By 1880, Chinese immigration had grown to over 100,000, which was relatively small in comparison with the numbers of Europeans who were arriving by that time. Chinese laborers were originally welcomed to work in the mines and lay railroad tracks, occupying positions in which American citizens were apparently unwilling to work for wages accepted by the Chinese. However, intense anti-Chinese feelings surfaced, particularly in the West. Resentment based upon racial, religious, economic, as well as language concerns culminated in the enactment of the Chinese Exclusion Act by the United States Congress in 1882, and further legislative restrictions specifically aimed at excluding Chinese immigrants. The constitutionality of this exclusion was upheld by the United States Supreme Court in 1889, with Mr. Justice Field writing:

> If therefore, the government of the United States, through its legislative department considers the presence of foreigners of a different race in this country, who will not assimilate with us to be dangerous to its peace and security, their exclusion is not to be stayed. . . . (*Chae Chan Ping* case, cited in the bibliography, at p. 606)

The anti-foreigner and anti-foreign language sentiment growing in the United States was not satisfied by the enactment and upholding of the Chinese Exclusion Act. Rather, the act and its endorsement by the U.S. Supreme Court gave new momentum to calls for further restriction with proposals for language restrictions occupying a prominent role. The perception that immigrants would cling to their native languages and fail to learn English was the subject of a literacy bill first introduced in the Congress in 1895. It failed, but led to new calls to make English ability a requirement for entry into this country. In 1906 a new English language requirement for obtaining citizenship was proposed and enacted.

In 1907 immigration to the United States reached a new high with the arrival of nearly 1.3 million immigrants. That year, Congress established a joint congressional commission to study the impact of immigration upon the United States. In 1909 the Dillingham Commission began its study. Relying upon the pseudoscientific theories of influential nativist scholars, it concluded in 1911 that new immigration was consisting largely of so-called inferior peoples, who were physically, mentally and linguistically different, and therefore less desirable than either the native born or early immigrant groups. It urged that as a result of the supposed inferiority, the United States should impose new

restrictions including literacy tests on entry of new immigrants. Presidential vetoes by Taft (1912) and Wilson (1915)
prevented congressionally approved literacy restrictions
from becoming law.

World War I heightened anxieties about loyalty and as-
similability of immigrants. Congress passed a new law
virtually banning all immigration from Asia and imposing
an entry literacy test. This time, Congress was able to
override the president's veto. Also, German-Americans,
who had been attacked by Franklin then later thought to be
among the most qualified immigrants, once again found
themselves the brunt of hostility. Several states prohibited
the teaching of German (see Chapter 2). The governor of
Iowa issued a decree prohibiting the use of any language
other than English in public places or over the telephone. A
similar proclamation was issued in South Dakota. Increasing hostility against German-Americans resulted in the
closing of German-language schools, social clubs and
newspapers.

It was also in this period that the Americanization movement sprang up. One government agency, the Bureau of
Naturalization, undertook a study to determine the extent
of immigrant education programs. Another, the Bureau of
Education pursued lobbying efforts that led twenty states
between 1919 and 1921 to enact legislation establishing
Americanization programs to insure that all immigrants
would learn English. The private sector also became involved with the Americanization movement. Ignorance of
English was considered an economic threat. Ford Motor
Company and International Harvester established English
language classes for their employees.

However, the movement to compel assimilation was not
succeeding, at least in the eyes of many. Foreign-speaking
language populations continued to exist within the United
States. The foreign language issue became tied up in the
rhetoric of anti-foreign sentiment. Nativists found support
in the earlier words of Theodore Roosevelt: "We have room
for but one language here and that is the English language,

for we intend to see that the crucible turns our people out as Americans, of American nationality, and not as dwellers in a polyglot boarding house" (Will). Because the literacy and language requirements in the existing immigration laws were not reducing the linguistic and cultural differences among the American population, a new restriction was proposed: limit immigration based upon the national origin of immigrants. In that fashion, it was proposed, the United States could limit immigration from countries which did not share our language, traditions and political system.

In 1921 Congress enacted a measure introducing the concept of national origin quotas to the nation's immigration laws. In 1924 a so-called permanent solution to U.S. immigration problems was enacted: the National Origins Act. The Act provided for an annual limit of 150,000 Europeans, a prohibition on immigration from Japan, and the development of quotas based on the contribution of each nationality to the existing United States population. It constituted, in the view of one commentator, "a rejection of one of the longest-lived democratic traditions of the United States, represented by George Washington's view that the United States should ever be an asylum to the oppressed and the needy of the earth. It also represented a rejection of cultural pluralism as a U.S. ideal. The Commissioner of Immigration could report, one year after this legislation took effect, that virtually all Americans looked exactly like Americans" (L. Fuchs in SCIRP, p. 197).

Despite the fact that immigration declined dramatically during and following the Great Depression, the United States policy of restrictive immigration continued. In 1939, for example, the U.S. Congress defeated a bill that would have rescued 20,000 children from Nazi Germany notwithstanding the willingness of American sponsors to provide for the children, on the grounds that such a large immigration would exceed the quota allotted to German immigration.

Following World War II, the nation's immigration restrictions were eased somewhat for a brief period of time. Mexico, which had seen its citizens welcomed as a cheap source of labor in the early 1900s, then expelled following the Depression, once again became a source of badly-needed inexpensive labor. The bracero program allowed temporary workers from Mexico into the United States. Congress also repealed the ban on Chinese immigration, reflecting this nation's new military alliance with China. The War Brides Act in 1946 permitted entry of 120,000 alien wives, husbands and children of members of the Armed Forces.

The Cold War brought new concerns. Refugees fleeing Communist countries were admitted. Other refugee acts followed although their impact was to supplement the quota system rather than to change it. The concern about Communist infiltration and menace in the 1950s led to the passage over President Truman's veto of the McCarran-Walter Bill. That act, which became known as the Immigration and Nationality Act, again contained national origin quotas. Truman considered them to be "utterly unworthy" of democratic traditions and ideals, and a violation of the humanitarian creed inscribed beneath the Statue of Liberty (U.S. Congress, House Document 520, 82nd Cong., 2d Sess., June 25, 1952).

Changes in the national origins quota system were not forthcoming until 1965. President Kennedy, who had once written a book denouncing the system, proposed legislation to abolish it. The effort eventually succeeded after his death. Immigration preference was to be based upon the goals of family reunification and work skills rather than national origin. However, even as the national origins formula was abolished, a limitation based upon hemispheric origin was imposed with the Western Hemisphere being afforded a smaller quota than the Eastern Hemisphere. This latter provision, which remained in effect until 1978, reflected the demographic reality that the proportion of Spanish-speaking citizens and immigrants was increasing in the United States. Lingering nativism was now becoming directed against immigrants from Mexico and Central

and South America. This time, following the established
tradition of the latest immigrant group bearing the brunt of
reprisals directed by earlier immigrants and their descendants, Spanish-speaking immigrants and citizens began to
feel the sting of immigration restrictions and public hostility directed at their language and culture. State legislative attempts, for example, sought to deny access to the
educational system and public benefits system to these
new arrivals and to their children. Repeated concern began
to be expressed that the country had lost control over its
borders, notwithstanding the fact that the percentage of
new immigrants to citizen population in the 1970s and
1980s was much smaller than in earlier periods of American
history. Oft-repeated concerns of language and loyalty surfaced again, with the rising use of Spanish being publicly
compared to the spread of a disease.

Repeated Congressional attempts to "regain control of
the borders" from the predominately Hispanic pool of undocumented aliens and would-be immigrants finally led to
the passage of the Immigration Reform and Control Act of
1986 (see Piatt, 63 Notre Dame L. Rev. at p. 35, 1988). The
act imposed sanctions for the first time upon employers
who hire undocumented workers and provided a limited
amnesty program for people who had successfully and
illegally run the gauntlet and established themselves in
American society. However, the act required proficiency in
English as a condition for permanent residence and eventual citizenship.

"Official English" Movement

A new reaction to language differences also arose. A
movement emerged in the United States seeking the passage of statutes and ultimately an amendment to the
United States Constitution that would make English the
official language of the country. In 1981, Senator S. I. Hayakawa introduced such an amendment. It was defeated. In

1984, another "official English" amendment was introduced as a joint resolution in the U.S. Congress. This time
the amendment was supported by U.S. English, a group
founded for that purpose by Hayakawa and Dr. John Tanton, a physician. A review of the record of the hearing on
this proposal before the Senate Committee on the Judiciary
reveals the familiar nativist concern that language minority
groups were not assimilating and therefore posed a threat
to the United States. The focus of the presentations in favor
of the amendment were clearly concerned with the rising
use of the Spanish language, and clearly unconcerned with
the Founding Fathers' notion that the cause of national
loyalty is served, rather than disserved, by leaving language choices to individuals and not public bodies. The
proposal died in committee.

A similar amendment was introduced in the Congress of
the United States in May 1988. Hearings on that proposed
bill continue as this book is being written. Again, concerns
are being raised by sponsors for maintenance of national
unity by imposition of a national language. One difference
between the 1988 proposal and the proposals of 1981 and
1984 is the recognition in the latest proposal of the continuing viability of educational instruction in a language other
than English to make students proficient in English. It also
would permit the teaching of foreign languages and the
use of court interpreters, as well as allowing for other laws
to protect public health or safety. Again, the thrust of the
measure appears to be concern over the increasing use of
Spanish. The legal and other bases for the "official English"
proposals are critiqued later in this book.

Proponents of these measures have also introduced and
obtained passage of constitutional amendments, statutes,
or resolutions making English the official language of the
respective states. A total of seventeen states now have
some form of "official English" law. Nine of those laws
were enacted between 1986 and 1988. Because ratification
of an "official English" constitutional amendment on the
federal level would require the approval of three-fourths of

the state legislatures (after passage by a two-thirds majority in both houses of Congress), it appears to be the strategy of proponents to obtain English statutes in most states, and then argue that ratification of the federal provision would be no major departure from existing state law. States with such provisions, and the year the law was enacted, include: Arizona (1988), Arkansas (1987), California (1986), Colorado (1988), Florida (1988), Georgia (1986—but Resolution never signed by Governor), Hawaii (1978—Hawaiian also official), Illinois (1923, amended 1969), Indiana (1984), Kentucky (1984), Mississippi (1987), Nebraska (1920), North Carolina (1987), North Dakota (1987), South Carolina (1987), Tennessee (1984), and Virginia (1981). Similar proposals have recently been defeated in the legislatures of Kansas and New Mexico.

However, the motives of the groups supporting such legislation have been questioned, and not just by their opponents. In October 1988, Walter Cronkite resigned from the board of U.S. English after learning of a memo by Dr. Tanton. The memo depicted an America possibly doomed to conflict between a minority of educated English speakers, and a majority of uneducated, poor people of ethnic and racial groups with faster population growth. Later in that month another board member, Linda Chavez, resigned after being told that major contributors to U.S. English advocated forced sterilization and other extraordinary positions in order to limit population and control immigration.

Viewed in a historical context, the feelings of U.S. English and similar groups and individuals today are perhaps no different from the feelings of earlier nativist groups and individuals. Even the tactic of employing state legislative Americanization remedies has its historical counterpart in a similar movement in the 1920s. What is different is the current movement's attempt to break with our centuries-old constitutional tradition of official linguistic neutrality. The groups favoring the "Official English" movement appear to be better financed and organized than early groups.

These changes may reflect the feeling that this is the last chance to limit the spread of Spanish in this country.

Counterpoint to the English-Only Movement: The Rebirth of Language Rights Consciousness

Recent political successes of the English-only movement have produced a new consciousness of the need to protect this nation's legal tradition regarding language rights. In August 1988, for example, the American Bar Association's house of delegates at their annual meeting in Toronto voted 200 to 132 to send back to committee for further study a resolution expressing disapproval of state and local laws aimed at establishing English as an official language. Proponents of the resolution contended that such laws convert lack of proficiency in the English language into a legal barrier to the enjoyment of equal rights, opportunities and government services. Eugene Thomas, past president of the American Bar Association, told the group that prohibiting the use of a language is the "ultimate attack on a culture, the ultimate weapon of oppression" (B.N.A. *Daily Report*, Aug. 16, 1988).

Other groups are springing up across the country to defend the recognition of language rights. Even though, for example, the Arizona English-only constitutional amendment passed, one group organized to oppose it was made up of Hispanics, Jews, Asians, Native Americans, and Anglo-Americans. It counted in its membership religious leaders, labor leaders, municipal officials, and state representatives. The group has continued beyond the ballot issue to educate the public of the dangers of the English-only movement and to provide literacy programs as well. The English Plus Information Clearing House is a coalition of national organizations with a center in Washington working to educate the public about the need to respect language rights.

A legislative response has also begun. In 1987 both

houses of the Louisiana Legislature unanimously adopted House Concurrent Resolution No. 21 supporting an amendment to the United States Constitution to protect the cultural rights of all Americans. The resolution, in relevant part, reads:

WHEREAS, America is a mosaic of peoples of many cultures proud of sharing a vast land in a spirit of freedom and tolerance of diversity; and

WHEREAS, the right of the people to preserve, foster, and promote their respective historic linguistic and cultural origins is recognized by the Constitution of Louisiana, but such recognition is under attack at the federal level and in other areas of the United States; and

WHEREAS, Senator John Breaux and Congressman Jimmy Hayes have introduced in the Congress of the United States a proposed constitutional amendment to protect the cultural rights of all Americans.

THEREFORE, BE IT RESOLVED that the Legislature of Louisiana does hereby memorialize the Congress of the United States to propose and submit to the states for ratification an amendment to the Constitution of the United States to protect the cultural rights of all Americans.

The Cultural Rights Amendment to which this resolution refers died in committee, but will apparently be reintroduced. That amendment reads:

The right of the people to preserve, foster, and promote their respective historic linguistic and cultural origins is recognized. No person shall be denied the equal protection of the laws because of culture or language. The Congress shall have the power to enforce this article by appropriate legislation.

In September 1988 Senator Inouye introduced a resolution "to establish as the policy of the United States the preservation, protection, and promotion of the rights of indigenous Americans to use, practice and develop Native American languages" (Sen. J.R. 379, 1988). It passed the

Senate on a voice vote, and was referred to the House Education and Labor Committee.

In the fall of 1988, a number of Texas legislators banded together to publicly announce that any legislative attempt to designate English as the official language of that state would be "dead on arrival."

In March 1989 the New Mexico Legislature passed a House Joint Memorial introduced by Speaker of the House Raymond Sanchez and others. That resolution, entitled, "Supporting Language Rights In the United States," provides, in part:

> WHEREAS, the people of New Mexico promote the spirit of diversity-with-harmony represented by the various cultures that make up the fabric of our state and American society; and
>
> WHEREAS, the people of New Mexico acknowledge that 'English Plus' best serves the national interest since it promotes the concept that all members of our society have full access to opportunities to effectively learn English plus develop proficiency in a second or multiple languages; and
>
> WHEREAS, the people of New Mexico recognize that the position of English in the United States needs no official legislation to support it; and
>
> WHEREAS, the people of New Mexico recognize that for survival in the twenty-first century our country needs both the preservation of the cultures and languages among us and the fostering of proficiency in other languages on the part of its citizens;
>
> NOW, THEREFORE, BE IT RESOLVED BY THE LEGISLATURE OF THE STATE OF NEW MEXICO that the first session of the thirty-ninth legislature of the state of New Mexico hereby reaffirms its advocacy of the teaching of other language in the United States and its belief that the position of English is not threatened. Proficiency on the part of our citizens in more than one language is to the economic and cultural benefit of our state and the nation, whether that proficiency derives from second language study by English speakers or from home language maintenance plus English acquisition by speakers of other languages. Proficiency in English plus other languages should be encouraged throughout the state.

Courts have also begun to be more explicit in identifying the basis for the need to protect language rights. The *Gutierrez* case discussed in Chapter 3 serves as an example of how courts will be able to identify the English-only statutes as assertions of pride in the English language that do not impede the rights of speakers of other languages to maintain their language and culture.

These legal developments parallel demographic data indicating that it is unlikely that the use of at least the Spanish language will be eradicated by the English-only movement.

Recent Growth of the Spanish Language

Studies demonstrate that most European immigrant groups in the United States did not pass on their language intergenerationally except in relatively limited numbers. Spanish is an obvious exception. A study by Macias (W. Connor, p. 287) in 1985 estimated there were at least 13.2 million Spanish speakers in this country representing almost a fourfold increase from the 3.3 million Spanish speakers estimated to exist in 1960 in the United States. Further, many factors suggest that Spanish will continue to be maintained as an important second language. Among the factors identified in a study by Gaarder (W. Connor, pp. 307–308) are the following.

First, Spanish speakers in the United States are the northernmost segment of more than 250 million Spanish speakers in Central and South America. Physical proximity to the motherland was not present with the immigration of other language groups. Second, most European immigrants tended to cluster in defined regions or ghettos. The large and growing size of the domestic Spanish-speaking population and the scattering of this large group throughout the country has given the United States Spanish-speaking population a national character. Third, partly as a result of continuing immigration and partly from internal migration, there is an intergenerational and interregional commingling that is tending to support language maintenance. Fourth, the development of an institutional language infrastructure has continued. Bilingual education has increased and Spanish continues to be the most popular foreign language in high schools and colleges.

Court decisions have enforced bilingualism in the areas of voting rights, court interpreters, and other important areas as later chapters in this book will discuss. The Spanish language mass media continues to grow. Univision, formerly the Spanish International Network, now counts more than 450 affiliated television stations providing twenty-four-hour Spanish language broadcasting in the United States. This number of affiliates has doubled in the last five years. Spanish language literature and cinema are experiencing a renaissance. Popular music in the United States indicates acceptance of Spanish themes.

In addition to factors identified in sociological studies, other language maintenance forces make it unlikely that Spanish will be assimilated. The growing economic and political strength of the Spanish-speaking population, for example, seem to guarantee further propagation and unofficial acceptance of the language in this country. Even as the English-only movement succeeds in state ballot initiatives, American industry increasingly appeals in Spanish, to consumers of Big-Macs, beer, children's cereals, and many other products. Assuming that a profit results from this advertisement, private promotion of the Spanish language should continue to increase. The 1988 presidential campaign produced the first bilingual national ticket, with Governor Dukakis and Senator Bentsen actively campaigning in Spanish as well as English. Not to be outdone, the son of the Republican standard-bearer appealed in Spanish during interviews on Univision and local media. Both tickets rejected English-only planks in their respective party platforms.

Continuing Presence of Other Languages

While the increasing presence of the Spanish language fuels the current debate, and while other languages may have assimilated to a greater extent than Spanish, it is important to consider the significant and continuing presence of foreign languages in use in the United States. The estimated 13.2 million Spanish speakers (1985) are joined by another 12 million Americans who, according to the 1980 census, come from homes where a language other than English or Spanish is spoken. These include German (1.6 million), French (1.6 million), Italian (1.6 million), Polish (820,000), Chinese (630,000), Philippine languages (474,000), Greek (402,000) and many others. In sum, more than 25 million Americans, representing more than ten percent of the total population of this country, currently speak a language other than English or come from a home where such a language is spoken.

The Future?

Predicting the future development of the legal recognition or limitation of language rights is risky business. This author obviously hopes that the future approach by courts and legislatures will be the analysis reflected in Chapters 9 and 10 of this book, and in the *Gutierrez* case (Chapter 3). For the immediate future, however, it seems reasonable to conclude, based upon recent political successes of the English-only movement, that its efforts to produce state English-only statutes and resolutions will succeed in perhaps another fifteen to twenty states. The movement probably will not, however, succeed in obtaining a federal constitutional amendment because of the heightened consciousness that this author hopes will result in part from this book. As a result, the state measures will not restrict any of the federally protected rights we will soon be examining in Chapter 2 through 7, at least where challenges to them are brought in the courts. This point, based upon the Supremacy Clause of the U.S. Constitution, is critical to remember as we approach a discussion of language rights.

In the meantime, as the debate continues, an important focus will likely be the issue of economics. English-only proponents will undoubtedly frame the issue as, "What does it cost us to produce bilingual ballots, educational materials, and otherwise render services in more than one language?" Such an approach, as discussed in Chapters 8 and 9, would ignore the costs to society of the failure to provide adequate language rights recognition, and the benefits that would otherwise accrue.

Courts, legislatures, and policymakers, including, most importantly, the body politic, will continue to be required to address other language issues, the complexities of which will become more apparent to the reader as we move into our discussions of the confusing and contradictory lines of language rights authorities. As we come to realize the important interests at stake, it may be that at some point in the future, state English-only laws will be viewed as historical curiosities, in the same category as laws prohibiting the teaching of foreign languages in the schools (struck down in 1923 by the *Meyer* case—see Chapter 2), or the San Francisco anti-queue ordinances which limited men's hair to one inch (struck down by the courts in the 1800s). At some point we might come to the recognition that the official exclusion of all but one tongue and the resulting resentment and discord may constitute a self-fulfilling prophecy creating linguistic and cultural friction, the prevention of which is supposedly the theoretical justification for English-only laws.

This historical introduction has admittedly been painted with a broad brush. The discussions in later chapters regarding the development of law and language in particular contexts will contain some further, although limited, historical considerations. Chapter 9 will provide a brief discussion of the evolution of language policies in other countries. The reader who seeks a deeper understanding of the historical forces shaping language development is encouraged to consult the bibliography, and the additional sources to which those materials refer.

With this background, we turn now to exploring the current legal recognition of a right to language in this country.

Bibliography

Books

1. T. Aleinikoff & D. Martin, *Immigration Process and Policy* (1985).
2. W. Beck, *New Mexico: A History of Four Centuries* (1962).
3. W. Beer and J. Jacob, eds., *Language Policy and National Unity* (1985).
4. J. Chambers, ed., *Black English, Educational Equity and the Law* (1983).
5. R. Clairborne, *Our Marvelous Native Tongue: The Life and Times of the English Language* (1983).
6. H. Commager, ed., *Immigration and American History* (1961).
7. N. Conklin & M. Lourie, *A Host of Tongues: Language Communities in the United States* (1983).
8. W. Connor, ed., *Mexican-Americans In Comparative Perspective* (1985).
9. V. Grove, *The Language Bar* (1950).
10. E. Hooglund, *Crossing the Waters* (1987).
11. New Mexico State Planning Office, *Land Title Study* (1971).
12. F. Orozco, *Historia de Mexico* (1982).

Articles

1. Cardenas, *United States Immigration Policy toward Mexico: An Historical Perspective*, 2 Chicano L. Rev. 66 (1975).
2. Heath, *A National Language Academy: Debate in the New Nation*, 11 Int'l. J. Soc. Language 9–44 (1976).

3. McClain, *The Chinese Struggle for Civil Rights in Nineteenth Century America: The First Phase,* 1850–1970, 72 Calif. L. Rev. 529 (1984).
4. Piatt, *Toward Domestic Recognition of a Human Right to Language,* 23 Hous. L. Rev. 885 (1986).
5. Piatt, *Born As Second Class Citizens In the U.S.A.: Children of Undocumented Parents,* 63 Notre Dame L. Rev. 35 (1988).
6. Will, *In Defense of the Mother Tongue,* Newsweek, July 8, 1985, p. 78.
7. Note, *"Official English": Federal Limits on Efforts to Curtail Bilingual Services in the States,* 100 Harv. L. Rev. 1345 (1987).
8. Note, *The Proposed English Language Amendment: Sword or Shield,* 3 Yale L. & Pol'y Rev. 519 (1985).

Constitutional Provisions and Statutes: English as Official Language

1. Arizona: Ballot referendum 11/8/88; to be codified at Ariz. Const. art. XXVIII.
2. Arkansas: Ark. Stat. Ann. § 1–4–117 (1987).
3. California: Cal. Const. art. III, § 6(b) (1988).
4. Colorado: Ballot referendum 11/8/88; to be codified at Colo. Const. art. II, § 30a.
5. Florida: Ballot referendum 11/8/88; to be codified at Fla. Const. art. II, § 9.
6. Georgia: House Resolution # 717, Act # 70 of the 1986 legislature; not signed by Governor.
7. Hawaii: Haw. Const. art. XV, § 4 (1985), Haw. Rev. Stat. § 1–13 (Hawaiian also official) (1985).
8. Illinois: Ill. Rev. Stat. ch. 1, para. 3005 (1980).
9. Indiana: Ind. Code Ann. § 1–2–10–1 (Burns 1987).
10. Kentucky: Ky. Rev. Stat. Ann. § 2.013 (Michie/Bobbs-Merrill 1985).
11. Mississippi: Miss. Code Ann. § 3–3–31 (1987).
12. Nebraska: Neb. Const. art. 1, § 27 (1985).
13. North Carolina: N.C. Gen. Stat. § 145–12 (1987).
14. North Dakota: N.D. Cent. Code § 54–02–13 (1987).
15. South Carolina: S.C. Code Ann. § 1–1–696 (Law. Co-op. 1987).

16.   Tennessee: Tenn. Code Ann. § 4–1–404 (1987).
17.   Virginia: Va. Code Ann. § 22.1–212.1 (1988).

Miscellaneous State Provisions

N.M. Const. art. XX, § 12 (publication of laws in English and
  Spanish); art. XII, § 8 (teachers to learn English and Spanish;
  but see Op. Att'y Gen. No. 68–15 and No. 71–102); art. XIX, § 1
  (publication of proposed const'l amendments in Spanish and
  English).
La. Const. art. I, § 3 (no discrimination permitted on basis of
  culture); La. Rev. Stat. Ann. § 17:272 (West 1982) (teaching of
  French language and culture and history of French population
  required in public schools).
Louisiana House Concurrent Resolution No. 21, by Mr. La-
  Londe, HLS 87–1158, Regular Session, 1987.
New Mexico House Joint Memorial No. 16, March, 1989.

Federal Statutes

1.   Chinese Exclusion Act of 1882, ch. 126, 22 Stat. 58 (1882).
2.   Displaced Persons Act of 1948, ch. 647, 62 Stat. 1009 (1948).
3.   Immigration and Nationality Act of 1952, 8 U.S.C. § 1101
      (1982).
4.   Immigration & Nationality Act Amendments of 1965.
5.   Immigration Reform & Control Act of 1986, Pub. L. No. 99–
      603, 100 Stat. 3359) (codified as amended in scattered
      sections of 7 U.S.C., 8 U.S.C., 18 U.S.C., 20 U.S.C., 29
      U.S.C., & 42 U.S.C.) (1986); Pub. L. No. 100–203, 101
      Stat. 1330 (current version at 42 U.S.C. § 673) (1987).
6.   National Origins Act of 1924, ch. 190, 43 Stat.. 153 (1924).
7.   Refugee Fair Share Law of 1960, Pub. L. No. 86–648, 74 Stat.
      504 (1960).

U.S. Supreme Court Cases

Chae Chan Ping v. United States, 130 U.S. 581 (1889) ("Chinese
  Exclusion" case) *Smith v. Turner,* 48 U.S. 283 (1849) (States may
  not regulate immigration).

Other Authorities

The English Language Amendment, 1984: Hearings on S.J. Res. 167 Before the Subcommittee on the Constitution of the Sen. Comm. on the Judiciary, 98th Cong., 2d Sess. (1984).

The English Language Amendment, 1988. Statement of Hon. Norman Shumway before the House Committee on the Jud. Subcommittee on Civil and Constitutional Rights, 5/11/88.

Select Commission on Immigration and Refugee Policy, Staff Report: *U.S. Immigration Policy and the National Interest*, L. Fuchs, S. Forbes, L. Koney, principal authors, pp. 123–232, 295–352 (April 30, 1981).

1980 U.S. Census, tables 183 (U.S. Summary 1–181 and 1–182), and 256 (U.S. Summary 1–16).

Bureau of the Census, U.S. Dep't of Commerce, Statistical Abstract of the United States 34 (1986).

Cultural Rights Amendment, S.J.R. 114 and H.C.R. 232 (1987).

Resolution of Senator Inouye and others re: Native American Languages, S.J.R. 379 (1988).

State-Local Government: ABA Meeting Split on Condemning State, Local English-Only Laws, *Daily Report for Executives, Regulation, Economics and Law,* The Bureau of National Affairs, Inc., August 16, 1988.

Ho Ah Kow v. Nunan, 5 Sawyer 552 (C.C.D. Cal. 1879) (invalidating San Francisco's queue ordinance), cited in T. Aleinikoff, p. 3 (1985).

Part Two

Evolution of the Contemporary Parameters of Language Rights

Chapter 2

Language Rights in the Classroom

We have already seen that there is no official language of this country and have examined some of the historical precedents for that position. As we begin to consider the development of language rights in various legal contexts, we confront another reality: there is no specific constitutional provision which, on its face, grants the right to communicate in foreign languages in the United States. Nonetheless, an examination of several cases in the educational context (and in later chapters as well), will illustrate how the courts have interpreted the Constitution to include such a right. We will also consider how rights created by statutes—that is, laws passed by the United States Congress and state legislatures—together with judicial decisions, have resulted in some guarantee that children, teachers, and parents share recognized and protected language rights in the educational arena, although the extent of that right is currently under debate.

Foundations of a Constitutional Right

Our historical discussion introduced us to the fact that German and things Germanic became the brunt of state legislative hostility during and following World War I. One expression of that hostility, and the nativist sentiment of the Americanization movement, was a series of statutes enacted in the states of Nebraska, Iowa, and Ohio aimed at prohibiting the teaching of the German language. The Nebraska statute, approved in April 1919, provided that no person should teach any subject, in any school, in any language other than English. It went on to provide that foreign languages could be taught, but only to pupils who had successfully passed the eighth grade. The law provided criminal penalties in the form of a misdemeanor violation. Persons violating the act could be fined not less than $25 and no more than $100, or be jailed for up to thirty days for each offense.

On May 25, 1920, a teacher at the Zion Parochial School in Hamilton County, Nebraska, taught reading in the German language to Raymond Parpart. Raymond was only ten years old and had not passed the eighth grade. The teacher, a Mr. Meyer, was charged, tried, and convicted under the Nebraska statute for unlawfully teaching in the German language. The readings he used in this process were a collection of biblical stories.

Meyer appealed his conviction to the Supreme Court of the state of Nebraska. He did not dispute that he had committed the acts as charged, but argued that the statute forbidding the teaching of German violated his rights to due process of law under the Fourteenth Amendment to the United States Constitution.

In order to understand the significance of the eventual outcome of this case and other principles at issue in the language rights debate, we must make a digression at this point. The Thirteenth, Fourteenth, and Fifteenth amendments to the United States Constitution were a direct outgrowth of the Civil War. The Thirteenth Amendment abolished slavery. The Fifteenth Amendment undertook to preserve the right to vote regardless of race, color, or previous condition of servitude. The Fourteenth Amendment became a tremendous constitutional pronouncement that has been described as bringing about a revolution in constitutional liberty. The major importance of the amendment turns on its language, "nor shall any state deprive any person of life, liberty, or property without due process of law; nor deny to any person within its jurisdiction the equal protection of the laws." Beginning in 1897, the United States Supreme Court began a gradual process of taking provisions from the Bill of Rights (the first ten amendments to the United States Constitution, applicable only to the federal government) and making them applicable to the states by reading them into the Fourteenth Amendment. The phrase "due process of law," which could well have been taken as applying only to guarantee fair criminal procedures, was construed to allow the court to begin the process of taking the guarantees of liberty in the Bill of Rights and making them applicable to the states. Also, although the words "due process of law" are not self-defining, the U.S. Supreme Court has long regarded as within its constitutional powers, the determination of the extent of the liberties and interests which would be protected against governmental interference by the use and application of that clause.

Let us return to Mr. Meyer's case. When Mr. Meyer pressed his argument in the Nebraska Supreme Court that the Fourteenth Amendment's due process clause protected his right to teach in the German language, notwithstanding the statute, the Nebraska Supreme Court disagreed and upheld his conviction. It concluded that rather than an infringement upon Mr. Meyer's due process rights, the application of the statute was a lawful exercise of the state of Nebraska's police power. It determined that the obvious purpose of the statute was that the English language should be and become the mother tongue of all children reared in the state. Citing similar decisions in Ohio and Iowa, it concluded that the enactment of such a statute came reasonably within the police power. The Nebraska Supreme Court noted that its legislature had seen "baneful effects" (*Meyer v. Nebraska*, 262 U.S. 390, 397 (1923)) of per-

mitting foreigners who had taken residence in this country
to rear and educate their children in their native languages.
It agreed with the legislature that the result of that condition was found to be "inimical to our own safety" (*Meyer* at
p. 398). It agreed with the legislature's apparent determination that allowing children of immigrants to be taught in
the language of the country of their parents would educate
them so that they would always think in that language,
and as a consequence, "naturally inculcate in them ideas
and sentiments foreign to the best interests of this country"
(*Meyer* at p. 398). The Nebraska Supreme Court went on to
note that a selection of subjects for the education of children is necessary given that the hours which a child is able
to devote to study are limited. It noted that many citizens
have never, except in rare instances, deemed it important
to teach their children foreign languages before the eighth
grade. The court upheld the constitutionality of the statute
and upheld Mr. Meyer's conviction.

Meyer was obviously not satisfied with the result and
pressed his claim to the United States Supreme Court. The
Supreme Court of the United States overturned his conviction. It found that the Nebraska statute (and others like it in
Iowa and Ohio) were unconstitutional. The Court determined that the right to teach a language and the rights of
parents to engage a teacher to so instruct their children are
among the liberties protected against infringement by the
Due Process Clause of the Fourteenth Amendment. The
Court's reasoning in this case is an important declaration of
the right to language in the educational context. First, the
Court noted that the liberty protected against infringement
by the Due Process Clause, while not exactly defined, de-
notes more than mere freedom from bodily restraint. It also
includes the right of the individual to engage in any of the
common occupations in life, to acquire useful knowledge,
to marry, establish a home and bring up children, to wor-
ship God, and generally enjoy "those privileges long recognized at common law as essential to the orderly pursuit
of happiness by free men" (*Meyer* at p. 399). The Court

noted that the American people have always regarded education and acquisition of knowledge as matters of supreme importance, and found that mere knowledge of the German language could not reasonably be regarded as harmful. In fact, the Court noted that, "heretofore it has commonly been looked upon as helpful and desirable" (*Meyer* at p. 400). The Court observed that Mr. Meyer taught this language in school as part of his occupation, concluding that his right thus to teach and the right of parents to engage him to instruct their children are within the due process liberties. Turning to the Nebraska Supreme Court's decision, the Court noted that while the state may go very far indeed to improve the quality of its citizens, the individual has certain fundamental rights which must be respected. It noted:

> the protection of the Constitution extends to all, to those who speak other languages as well as to those born with English on the tongue.

(Author's note: Obviously, no child is born with English or any other language on his or her tongue.) The Court went on:

> Perhaps it would be highly advantageous if all had ready understanding of our ordinary speech, but this cannot be coerced by methods which conflict with the Constitution—a desirable end cannot be promoted by prohibited means.

The Court found there would be power in the state to make reasonable regulations for all schools including a requirement that they give instruction in English, but found no emergency which rendered knowledge by a child of some language other than English so clearly harmful as to justify its inhibition. The Court concluded:

> It is well known that proficiency in a foreign language seldom comes to one not instructed at an early age and experience shows that this is not injurious to the health, morals, or understanding of the ordinary child.

The *Meyer* decision of the United States Supreme Court has never been overturned.

What if the issue is not whether an English-speaking child can be taught in a foreign language, but rather whether a non-English-speaking child can be taught in the child's mother tongue while he or she acquires a command of the English language? Again, broadly speaking, there is such a right, although the bases for it and the extent of it are not as clear as in the *Meyer* circumstances. These concerns are lumped together in current legal and educational thought, under the label of bilingual education—the topic to which we now turn.

Bilingual Education Statutes

The dramatic rise in the Spanish-speaking population, particularly school age children, following World War II led to an increasing debate about the education of language minority children in the nation's school system. Not only were foreign languages often ignored in the curriculum, indeed, many children, particularly Hispanics, can recall days when they were punished, often physically, for speaking Spanish at school. Beyond the language punishment issue, other indicators of second-class status were communicated to Spanish-speaking students. A distinguished New Mexico jurist, for example, recalls being taken to the school's showers for cleaning up with other Spanish-speaking students, a so-called opportunity not given to his English-speaking Anglo-American peers.

Various groups and individuals in the 1960s sought federal legislation that would guarantee respect for the Spanish-speaking child's cultural heritage while at the same time enabling the child to gain further proficiency in Spanish and English. They were joined by others who saw a bilingual education statute as the most effective method for producing English-proficient children among language minority populations. The congressional response was the

Bilingual Education Act of 1968 which provided grants to promote research and experimentation for meeting the needs of children who demonstrated little or no proficiency in the English language. In 1970 another important legal source of bilingual education was opened to language minority students. In that year, the Health Education and Welfare Department of the United States enacted a regulation pursuant to Title VI of the Civil Rights Act of 1964. The Civil Rights Act of 1964 provides in part that:

> No person in the United States shall, on the basis of race, color, or national origin, be excluded from participation in, be denied the benefits of, or be subjected to discrimination under any program or activity receiving federal financial assistance.

The 1970 regulation, enacted pursuant to congressional power under the Civil Rights Act, provided:

> Where inability to speak and understand the English language excludes national origin minority group children from effective participation in the educational program offered by a school district, the district must take affirmative steps to rectify the language deficiency in order to open its instructional program to these students.

Following the decision of the United States Supreme Court in the *Lau* case (discussed below), the United States Congress also passed the Equal Educational Opportunity Act in 1982. Included in the provisions of that act is the following:

> No state shall deny equal educational opportunity to an individual on account of his or her race, color, sex, or national origin, by . . . (f) the failure by an educational agency to take appropriate action to overcome language barriers that impede equal participation by its students in instructional programs.

A number of states have enacted their own bilingual educational provisions. A listing of those laws appears in

the bibliography. One writer, Moran, notes that state bilingual education acts generally declare the state's commitment to meeting the needs of students who either do not
speak English or who have limited proficiency in that language. The laws then provide for the identification and
assessment of these students, describe the types of programs the state will utilize to meet these needs, set forth
requirements for staffing and parental involvement, and
authorize state funding.

Judicial Decisions Concerning Bilingual Education

In addition to proposals for legislation, parents of language minority children began pressing demands in the
courts for bilingual education. One early and significant
case was filed in the United States District Court for the
District of New Mexico. In that case, *Serna v. Portales Municipal Schools*, the plaintiffs were Spanish-surnamed minors
represented by their parents. They claimed that unlawful
discrimination against them resulted from the defendants'
educational program tailored to educate a middle-class
child from an English-speaking family without regard for
the educational needs of the child from an environment
where Spanish is the predominant language. They based
their claims on Title VI of the Civil Rights Act (see above)
and also alleged deprivation of due process and equal protection guaranteed by the Fourteenth Amendment of the
United States Constitution.

A number of expert witnesses explained the impact upon
children of the rejection of their language and culture. A Dr.
Zintz testified that when Spanish-surnamed children come
to school and discover that their language and culture are
totally rejected and that only English is acceptable as a
means of communication, feelings of inadequacy and lower
self-esteem develop. The director of the Communicative
Arts division of the New Mexico Department of Education,

Mr. Henry Pasqual, testified that a child who goes to school where there is no evidence of his or her language, culture, and ethnic group represented becomes withdrawn. Maria Gutierrez Spencer, a New Mexico teacher, testified that until a child developed a good self-image, not even teaching English as a second language would be successful. She also concluded that, on the other hand, a child who is made to feel worthwhile in school will learn even with a poor English program. Dr. Estevan Moreno, a psychologist, explained that children who are not achieving often demonstrate both academic and emotional disorders. Thrusting Spanish-surnamed students into an alien school environment produces frustration. This is expressed in irregular attendance, lack of school involvement, and minimal community involvement. The frustrations are reflected further in hostile behavior and discipline problems and eventually result in the student dropping out of school.

The trial judge, District Judge Edwin Mechem, found the defendants violated the constitutionally guaranteed equal protection rights of the plaintiffs. He ordered, among other remedies, that defendants provide bilingual and bicultural instruction and seek funding under the federal and state bilingual education acts for that instructional program. The defendants appealed. On appeal, the Tenth Circuit Court of Appeals found that the district court had reached the correct result and affirmed the remedial steps ordered by that court. However, it chose not to reach the equal protection issue. Rather, it chose to follow the approach adopted by the United States Supreme Court in the case of *Lau v. Nichols. Lau* was decided in 1974, after the district court decision in the *Serna* case. In *Lau*, Chinese-speaking plaintiffs alleged the public school system in San Francisco schools denied them an education because the only classes offered were in the English language. *Lau* found a deprivation of statutory rights under Title VI of the Civil Rights Act of 1964 and the HEW regulations requiring school systems to take remedial steps to rectify language deficiency problems (see above). In *Serna*, the Tenth Circuit applied this *Lau*

approach and affirmed on statutory grounds the court-
ordered bilingual education plan imposed by Judge Mechem. As a result of *Lau, Serna,* and other cases (some cited
in the bibliography), the courts have upheld the existence
of statutory and regulatory rights to that form of education,
though it cannot be firmly stated that there is a constitutional right to bilingual education.

In addition to identifying the source of a right to bilingual education, courts are often faced with determining
the type and extent of the program to which language
minority students are entitled. In *Serna,* the district judge
imposed, and the appellate court upheld, an extensive
program incorporating the classic bilingual-bicultural approach. At the elementary school in Portales, New Mexico,
with the highest concentration of Spanish-speaking students, the court required a minimum of sixty minutes per
day of bilingual education for grades 1 through 3, and
forty-five minutes per day for grades 4 through 6. At three
other elementary schools with a lesser Spanish-speaking
enrollment, thirty minutes per day of bilingual instruction
was ordered for students in grades 1 through 6. The court
required a bicultural outlook incorporated in as many subject areas as possible in the elementary schools with sup-
plemental bilingual education available as necessary in the
school system. Further, the court required the offering of
an elective ethnic studies course at the high school level.
These remedies were clearly aimed at achieving more than
minimal English proficiency; rather, they sought to promote substantive learning in the mother tongue and acceptance of the language and culture of the minority students.

In *Lau,* however, the Supreme Court left the task of
designing a remedy to local officials. It noted that even
though plaintiffs sought no specific remedy, teaching English to students of Chinese ancestry who do not speak the
language would be one alternative. Instructing this group
in substantive courses using the Chinese language would
be another. And the court noted the existence of other
possible remedies. As a result, we cannot firmly identify a

constitutional right to bilingual education, nor can we clearly identify an absolute statutory or regulatory right to subject matter instruction in a native tongue. Nor can we find a requirement, unless imposed by state statute or a court, for a multicultural approach designed to promote acceptance of the minority culture. What we can say is that Title VI, as implemented by regulation, requires districts to take "affirmative steps to rectify the language deficiency in order to open its instructional program" (*Lau v. Nichols*, 414 U.S. 563, 568 (1974) citing the regulation at 35 Fed. Reg. 11595) to language minority students. Also, the Equal Educational Opportunity Act requires that an educational agency take "appropriate action to overcome language barriers that impede equal participation by its students" (20 U.S.C. § 1703 (f)). Courts can, in appropriate cases, fashion broad bilingual-bicultural programs when local school districts violate these federal provisions and accompanying regulations. School districts themselves are permitted under federal law, and required under some state laws, to create and implement their own bilingual-bicultural programs to meet the needs of their language minority students. However, absent a state provision or a court order requiring the full traditional bilingual-bicultural approach, school districts are legally permitted to select other options, although as noted below, the bulk of federal funding is awarded to bilingual (traditional or transitional) programs.

A brief discussion of the options might be helpful at this point. We have identified the *traditional* bilingual education approach, with substantive learning in the mother tongue, and continuing *bicultural* approaches such as ethnic studies or foreign language maintenance classes (*Serna*). *Transitional* bilingual education provides subject matter instruction in the mother tongue and English language instruction but only for the minimal amount of time necessary for the student to learn English. (This may be the approach in the latest proposed U.S. constitutional amendment.) Other options provide for no substantive teaching in the native tongue and have been compared to a sink-or-swim approach. *Structured immersion* programs have a bilingual teacher teaching the classes in English, although at least at first, children may ask questions in the native tongue. Others use an *English as a Second Language* approach, with minority children receiving all substantive instruction in English, supplemented only by an additional English language class, notwithstanding the conclusion of many experts and some courts that teaching the language minority child exclusively in English communicates a powerful message to the child that he or she is a second-class citizen.

Continuing Debate over the Extent of the Right to Bilingual Education

Not everyone is content with even the limited right to bilingual education in this country. Former Secretary of Education, William Bennett, for example, in a September 26, 1985, address to the Association for a Better New York, decried the view, as he perceived it, that bilingual education programs were fostering cultural pride at the price of proficiency in English. He also objected to the 1984 congressional limitation of four percent of the bilingual education allocation for English as a Second Language or structured immersion programs. He found no evidence that children had benefited from the $1.7 billion which Congress had, to that point, allocated to bilingual education. And he took exception to the fact that the congressional allocation in 1984 for the first time authorized funding for programs designed to maintain student competence in the native language.

Position papers of U.S. English and other testimony introduced by supporters of an "official English" constitutional amendment make abundantly clear that the concept of educating children in another tongue is one of the key targets of the English-only movement. Bilingual education would be replaced with English language acquisition classes. Bicultural education would be removed from the public schools. A two-year limit upon English acquisition for children would be imposed, all as set forth in a fact sheet of U.S. English dated April 11, 1984.

With the limited but nonetheless basic legal structure in place, it is unlikely that there will be any successful attack upon the basic right of minority language students to receive some form of bilingual education in the future. Rather, it appears the battle lines will be drawn over the form such education should take, with the debate continuing over the level of funding of the classic bilingual-bicultural approach or transitional program, as opposed to the sink-or-swim approaches. In appropriate cases, courts will be urged to select among these forms and to impose remedies for failure of local school districts to provide "affirmative steps to rectify the language deficiency" (Title VI), or "appropriate action to overcome language barriers" (Equal Educational Opportunity Act), or similar language in state statutes. In these debates, opponents of the bilingual-bicultural approach will press the argument by Bennett and others that, in effect, quick, unilingual mainstreaming should be both the ends and the means toward national linguistic unity.

Proponents of a broader approach to the issue may wish to consider, in addition to the testimony previously noted, the studies of Hakuta and Campbell. Their reports, summarized in the "Washington Update of the Consortium of Social Science Associations" on March 22, 1985, refer to empirical evidence for the value of bilingual education in providing language minority students with the acquisition of substantive knowledge and English proficiency, and allowing native English speakers the desirable opportunity to acquire second language skills. They conclude that the traditional bilingual-bicultural education in fact provides for rapid transition to English. They note that research in second language acquisition actually argues in favor of prolonging the period in which students receive instruction in their native language. Skills such as reading transfer from one language to another so that a student is not learning to read in the native language at the expense of reading in English. They note a great variation in the rate at which different children learn a second language depending on personality, aptitude, and other factors. They conclude it would be wise to allow a more comfortable period for English development to take place, because recent research shows that the use of language in academic learning is different from language used in conversation and takes considerably longer to develop.

Hakuta and Campbell also conclude that research supports maintenance bilingual programs. In such a program, the student is encouraged to maintain the mother language. Research shows that fully functional bilingualism can be attained at no expense to English. Hakuta and Campbell point to research showing it is wrong to think of two languages of the bilingual speaker in competition for limited mental space. Rather, they are interdependent and build upon each other. Bilingual children demonstrate not only the benefits of knowing two languages and literatures, but added cognitive skills and awareness about language as well. Studies conducted at the turn of the century on immigrants concluded that bilingualism results in mental confusion. Similar studies also concluded that representatives of one particular ethnic group could never make good Boy Scouts, and that another group was prone to criminality. These studies have long been debunked.

Hakuta and Campbell note another lesson to be learned from bilingual education. That is, a second language is learned well when effectively integrated into other areas of the curriculum. They point to success in a San Diego study, where English speakers who wanted to learn Spanish were taught in classes which used Spanish as a medium of substantive instruction. At the same time, the school interlocked the program with an ongoing bilingual program for native speakers of Spanish so that the two groups of students serve as linguistic resources for each other.

Proponents of traditional bilingual education might want

to consider another source in the ongoing legal/sociological/political debate over bilingual education. Professor Baral identifies the earliest version of the native language hypothesis as the UNESCO conference of 1951 resulting in a publication entitled "The Use of Vernacular Languages in Education" (UNESCO, 1953). The authors of the publication stated, "We take it as axiomatic . . . that the best medium for teaching is the mother tongue of the child." The basic argument can be summarized in four postulants:

1. Every child should begin schooling in the home language and should continue receiving instruction in that language as long as possible.
2. There are no inferior languages; any language can be used for elementary education.
3. Higher education in vernacular language is strongly recommended, although it is recognized that some languages will require vocabulary development in technical fields.
4. If the child's first language is not the national language of a country, or a world language, then that child should learn a second language.

Professor Baral identifies criticism of the statement but concludes that it has been incorporated into the rationale for bilingual education in the United States, citing the U.S. Commission on Civil Rights, 1975, and other sources. In the current debate, opponents of bilingual education have, in essence, focused only on the fourth of these postulates.

Another study by M. Tienda and L. Nidert published in 1985 found no basis for assuming that bilingual education programs which encourage retention of Spanish among Hispanics will necessarily retard their socioeconomic success. Their results suggested that foreign-born workers could improve their occupational status by participating in bilingual education programs, although it was unclear how much emphasis would need to be placed on improving English language skills and how much would be necessarily devoted to teaching basic skills in reading, arithmetic, and communication in order to produce desired outcomes. They found that bilingual education programs should not be geared to eliminating the use of Spanish, because among natives who tend to have a better command of English, Spanish bilingualism does not depress socioeconomic achievement.

Another argument in favor of the maintenance of the mother tongue in bilingual education is the reality, as noted in *Meyer*, that the presence of other languages is generally thought to be helpful and desirable rather than harmful. Indeed our school systems teach and often require foreign languages. (We have also seen several instances where the presence of other tongues served the military interests of this country.) The question might be raised as to what interests are served by attempting to push other languages out of the minds of our children, and then attempting to push them back in again years later? Additional studies, and questions, are presented in the material listed in the bibliography.

Additional Legal Considerations

As the debate over the existence, type, and extent of bilingual education programs continues, there are additional legal issues that will need to be examined. For example, while there has been no clear pronouncement up to this point that there is a right on a constitutional basis to bilingual education, removing language maintenance programs from language minority students in order to cause them to acquire English proficiency while losing mother tongue proficiency could arguably run afoul of *Meyer*. That is, while it is reasonable for the state to include a requirement that children be given instruction in English, there is no emergency which renders continuing knowledge by a child of his or her mother tongue so clearly harmful as to justify its inhibition in state-supported educational programs.

Another potential source of legal controversy is the fact that four years after the *Lau* decision, the U.S. Supreme Court held in a reverse discrimination case, the *Bakke* case, that Title VI embodies certain constitutional principles. Whether a constitutional right to bilingual education might thus be inferred is open to debate. Such a reading would find difficulty, however, in the fact that as the U.S. Supreme Court has noted (*San Antonio Independent School District v. Rodriguez,* 1973) education itself is not a fundamental right. In a further twist, the U.S. Supreme Court ruled in the *Plyler v. Doe* case in 1982 that even though there is no constitutional right to an education, where the state provides public schooling it cannot, consistent with the Equal Protection Clause of the Fourteenth Amendment, deny access to those schools to children who are not legally admitted into the U.S. It would follow, that if those undocumented children do not happen to speak English, one might then infer some constitutional basis for some form of bilingual education.

Another potential recurring legal issue is the applicability of the bilingual education laws to speakers of Black English. A 1979 decision by the United States District Court for the Eastern District of Michigan found that the Equal Educational Opportunities Act of 1974 applies in that setting as well as in the foreign language setting. The court in that case noted that Black English is and has been used at some time by eighty percent of the black people in this country and has as its genesis the transactional or pidgin language of the slaves which, after a generation or two, became a Creole language. Expert testimony indicated that black children who succeed learn to be bilingual, retaining fluency in Black English to maintain status in the community, and becoming fluent in standard English to succeed in the general society. The children learn to code switch from one to the other as do bilingual children, depending on the circumstances. Evidence presented indicated that teaching effective code switching to children was complex. Some of the experts suggested that children's speech not be corrected initially until the correction could be made without upsetting the child and the feelings toward mother and home. Insensitive teachers, it was found, who treat the children's language system as inferior, can create a barrier in these children, preventing them from learning to read and use standard English. As a result, the court ordered the Ann Arbor school district to prepare a plan, subject to court approval, to help teachers identify children speaking Black English and to use that knowledge in teaching such students how to read standard English. The case, cited in the bibliography, contains a summary of resources and materials regarding Black English. One difference in these cases as opposed to the foreign language bilingual cases is that plaintiffs are apparently not urging the maintenance of Black English.

The nature and extent of a right to language in the classroom will continue to constitute an important focus of the language rights debate. It is particularly important, given the impact the outcome will have upon the segment of society arguably least able to protect its interests: children. The results will undoubtedly have a profound effect upon the continuing development of the law in other language contexts, as those children who have received societal signals as to whether they and their native tongues and cultures were acceptable bring their feelings and their language abilities into, or away from, our mainstream.

Bibliography

Books

1. N. Appleton, *Cultural Pluralism in Education* (1983).
2. J. Fishman & G. Keller, eds., *Bilingual Education for Hispanic Students in the United States* (1982).
3. M. Gordon, *Assimilation in American Life* (1964).

4. G. Guthrie, *A School Divided: An Ethnography of Bilingual Education in a Chinese Community* (1985).
5. G. Keller, R. Teschner, & S. Viera, eds., *Bilingualism in the Bicentennial and Beyond* (1976).
6. E. Murguia, *Assimilation, Colonialism and the Mexican-American People* (1975).
7. R. Samuda & S. Kong, *Multicultural Education: Programmes and Methods* (1986).

Articles

1. Avila, *Equal Educational Opportunities for Language Minority Children*, 55 U. Colo. L. Rev. 559 (1984).
2. Guzman, *Dando Fin a las Angustias del Pasado*, El Visitante Dominical (Nov. 10, 1985).
3. Haft, *Assuring Equal Educational Opportunity for Language-Minority Students: Bilingual Education and the Equal Educational Opportunity Act of 1974*, 18 Colum. J. L. & Soc. Probs. 209 (1983).
4. Hakuta and Campbell, *The Future of Bilingual Education*, C.O.S.S.A., Washington Update, Consortium of Social Science Associations (Mar. 22, 1985).
5. Kobrick, *A Model Act Providing for Transitional Bilingual Education Programs in Public Schools*, 9 Harv. J. Legis. 260 (1972).
6. Moran, *Bilingual Education as a Status Conflict*, 75 Calif. L. Rev. 321 (1987).
7. Piatt, *Born as Second Class Citizens in the U.S.A.: Children of Undocumented Parents*, 63 Notre Dame L. Rev. 35 (1988).
8. Piatt, *Toward Domestic Recognition of a Human Right to Language*, 23 Hous. L. Rev. 885 (1986).
9. Tienda & Neidert, *Language, Education, and the Socioeconomic Achievement of Hispanic Origin Men*, in the Mexican American Experience 374 (1985).

Federal Constitutional Provisions, Statutes, and Regulations

U.S. Const. amends. V, XIII, XIV, & XV.
Bilingual Education Act of 1968, 20 U.S.C. §§ 3221–3262 (1982).

Equal Educational Opportunity Act, 20 U.S.C. § 1701 (1982).
Civil Rights Act of 1964, 42 U.S.C. § 2000a (1981).
Office for Civil Rights Notice, 35 Fed. Reg. 11595 (1970); 45 C.F.R.
  § 80 (1986).

Selected Federal Judicial Decisions

1. *Chicago, Burlington, and Quincy R.R. Co. v. Chicago,* 166 U.S.
   226 (1897).
2. *Lau v. Nichols,* 414 U.S. 563 (1974).
3. *Meyer v. Nebraska,* 262 U.S. 390 (1923).
4. *Plyler v. Doe,* 457 U.S. 202 (1982).
5. *San Antonio Indep. School Dist. v. Rodriguez,* 411 U.S. 1 (1973).
6. *University of Cal. Regents v. Bakke,* 438 U.S. 265 (1978).

Other Cases (Only a few of the many reported cases are included here, because of space limitations.)

1. *Guadalupe Org. v. Tempe Elementary School Dist.,* 587 F.2d
   1022 (9th Cir. 1978).
2. *Martin Luther King Jr. Elem. School Children v. Ann Arbor
   School Dist. Bd.,* 473 F. Supp. 1371 (E.D. Mich. 1979).
3. *Serna v. Portales Mun. Schools,* 351 F. Supp. 1279 (D. N.M.
   1972), *aff'd,* 499 F.2d 1147 (10th Cir. 1974).
4. *United States v. Texas,* 506 F. Supp. 405 (E.D. Tex. 1981),
   rev'd, 680 F.2d 356, 372 (5th Cir. 1982).

State Bilingual Education Statutes

1. Alaska Stat. § 14.30.400 (1975).
2. Ariz. Rev. Stat. Ann. § 15–752 (1984).
3. Cal. Educ. Code § 52160 (West 1981).
4. Colo. Rev. Stat. § 22–24–101 (1987).
5. Conn. Gen. Stat. Ann. § 10–17a (West 1986).
6. Del. Code Ann. tit. 14, § 122 (1987).
7. Ill. Rev. Stat. ch. 122, para. 14C–1 (1973).

8. Ind. Code § 20–10.1–5.5 (1976).
9. Kan. Stat. Ann. § 72–9501 (1985).
10. La. Rev. Stat. Ann. §§ 17:272, 17:273 (West 1982).
11. Me. Rev. Stat. Ann. tit. 20A, § 4602(3) & (4) (1983) (repealed 1983).
12. Mass. Gen. Laws Ann. ch. 71 (West 1971).
13. Mich. Stat. Ann. § 15.41152 (Callaghan 1987).
14. Minn. Stat. § 126.262 (1988).
15. N.H. Rev. Stat. Ann. § 189:19 (1987).
16. N.J. Rev. Stat. Ann. § 18A:35–15 (West 1988).
17. N.M. Stat. Ann. § 22–23–1 (1978).
18. N.Y. Educ. Law § 3204 (McKinney 1981) (amended 1988).
19. Pa. Stat. Ann. tit. 24, § 15–1511 (Purdon 1988).
20. R.I. Gen. Laws § 16–54 (1987).
21. Tex. Educ. Code Ann. § 21.451 (Vernon 1987).
22. Wash. Rev. Code Ann. § 28A.58.800 (1982 & supp. 1989).
23. Wis. Stat. Ann. § 115.95 (West 1988).

Other Authorities

Address by William J. Bennett, U.S. Secretary of Education, to Assoc. for a Better New York, September 26, 1985.

Hearings on the English language Amendment, 1984 (cited following Chapter 1 of this book).

UNESCO, *The Use of Vernacular Languages in Education* (1953), reprinted in Baral, *Second Language Acquisition Theories Relevant to Bilingual Education,* in *Theory, Technology, and Public Policy on Bilingual Education* (1983).

Chapter 3

The Workplace

Another important area where law and language issues arise is the workplace. Misconceptions about the applicability of state English-only laws add to the complexity of these questions. In general, courts find that discrimination in employment matters based upon language is impermissible national origin discrimination unless there is some legitimate reason for it. Courts, then, are required to determine whether the alleged business reasons are legitimate, and if so, to balance them against the language rights of workers. The legal provisions and procedures involved are complex. Misconceptions on the part of employers that state English-only laws give them some greater rights in imposing language restrictions often add to the confusion. (These misconceptions should be cleared up as a result of a 1988 decision of the U.S. Ninth Circuit Court of Appeals, discussed in this chapter, which cites this author's 1986 Houston Law Review article and other authorities for the proposition that broad English-only work rules cannot be enforced.)

In this chapter, we consider how the courts have struck a balance in several areas. First, we consider whether it is permissible for an employer to discriminate in hiring based upon English language ability or the presence of a foreign language accent. Second, assuming that a person with foreign language ability is hired, to what extent does the employee have the right to use that language on the job? The balancing is not limited, however, to the interests of employer and employee. In a third section we will examine how the courts react when an employee asserts that his or her union must provide language assistance to enable the employee to participate in union activities.

Discrimination in Hiring Based Upon Language or Accent

There are two important federal statutes which protect the right of a worker to be free from discrimination regarding employment matters. Title VII of the Civil Rights Act of 1964, 42 U.S.C. § 2000e (Equal Employment Opportunity Act) prohibits employment discrimination on the basis of race, color, religion, sex, or national origin. The Equal Employment Opportunity Commission (EEOC), an administrative body created by the act, is charged with enforcing it. Both the EEOC and the courts have agreed that language rights at the workplace are protected under the national origin pigeonhole. (Protecting language rights under a national origin theory is also discussed in Chapter 5 of this book, and critiqued in Chapter 10.) Courts have also recognized that another statute, 42 U.S.C. § 1981, provides a parallel remedy to the Equal Employment Opportunity Act on the issue of language rights in employment. That act is part of a number of civil rights laws passed by Congress following the Civil War. We will examine cases and proceedings brought under these provisions in a language rights context.

Equal Employment Opportunity Act

By way of a brief introduction to understanding the application of these provisions, Title VII was intended to assure equality of employment opportunities, eradicate discrimination in employment, and make the victims of employment discrimination whole. Proscribed discrimination is not limited to discrimination in hiring, firing, or the payment of wages, but includes discriminatory terms and conditions of employment. Title VII prohibits not only intentional discrimination with respect to conditions of employment, but also facially neutral rules which have a disparate impact on protected groups of workers. A rule that appears facially neutral which nonetheless falls more harshly on a protected group (such as Hispanics) violates Title VII unless it is justified by a business necessity. A rule or practice that is adopted for the *purpose* of discriminating against a protected group violates the statute unless it meets the stricter bona fide occupational qualification test.

In an early case, decided June 30, 1969, the EEOC determined that reasonable cause existed to believe that an employer violated the Equal Employment Opportunity Act when a new branch manager of a printing facility fired a typesetter for alleged incompetency on the basis of a language problem. The new branch manager identified the reason for the firing as the employee "not being able to speak, read, and understand English very well" (2 Fair Empl. Prac. Cas. (BNA) No. YAU 9–048 at 78). The difficulty with the employer's position, from the viewpoint of the Equal Employment Opportunity Commission, was that the typesetter had acquired more than sixteen years experience as a typesetter, implicitly requiring the ability to communicate effectively in English, as of the time of his firing by a new branch manager in January 1968. Court decisions also began to recognize that discrimination against an employee or potential employee because of a foreign language background would constitute unlawful national origin discrimination under the Equal Employment Opportunity Act. One relatively early case setting forth this principle is the case of *Jones v. United Gas*, a 1975 federal district court case in Pennsylvania.

This protection against discrimination based upon foreign language ability even extends to protect persons with a foreign accent which does not interfere with their ability to perform duties, from adverse employment decisions. This principle was set down in a 1974 case decided by the United States Circuit Court of Appeals for the Tenth Circuit, in a case entitled *Carino v. University of Oklahoma Board of Regents*. In that case, Mr. Carino was hired by the defendants as supervisor of a dental laboratory at the University of Oklahoma College of Dentistry. The court found that Mr. Carino's demotion from these duties resulted from the opinion held by certain dental college faculty that the plaintiff was unsuitable to continue as supervisor because of his national origin (Republic of the Philippines) and his related accent. Because there was no showing that his accent interfered with his duties, the court concluded that a showing had been made of unlawful national origin discrimination.

These cases, however, do not stand for the broad proposition that no employer may ever decline to offer employment or promotions to someone with limited English ability. Language difficulties that interfere with the performance of duties may be legitimately considered in employment decisions. In the case, for example, of a chambermaid seeking promotion to a front office job in a hotel, a federal district court in New York held in a 1978 decision that no showing of discrimination had been made. The chambermaid's limited ability to speak English would preclude her from satisfactorily working in an office setting, although it did not preclude her from performing her duties as a maid. In 1989, the U.S. Ninth Circuit Court of Appeals upheld a decision not to hire as a clerk a man whose Filipino accent was so heavy it would have a deleterious effect upon his ability to communicate orally with 200–300 disgruntled members of the public each day.

Similarly, one could conceive of other situations where an employee's foreign language accent would be so strong as to interfere with the ability to perform duties. One example might be a position as a dispatcher for a local police department, where the ability to quickly and clearly communicate might be necessary for the prevention of injury and damage to person and property. In such a case, courts would probably allow the employer to deny employment or deny promotions to someone whose accent or language difficulties rendered job performance unsatisfactory.

However, given that the EEOC and the courts have now established the principle that discrimination based upon language can constitute unlawful discrimination based upon national origin under Title VII, an employer will have to offer some legitimate, nondiscriminatory reason for the practice of limiting employment to those proficient in English or run the risk of being held liable for a violation of the rights of non-English speaking employees and potential employees. Even if the employer offers a facially legitimate, nondiscriminatory reason for the language discrimination, an employee or potential employee would still be given a final opportunity in court to show that the employer's reason is merely a pretext for unlawful discrimination. The employee would succeed in this endeavor either by directly persuading the court that a discriminatory reason motivated the employer, or by indirectly showing that the employer's explanation is unworthy of credence. As a result, an employer who wishes to impose broad English proficiency requirements upon workers will still have a difficult time escaping liability under Title VII, notwithstanding the recent relaxation by the U.S. Supreme Court of an employer's burden of proof in disparate impact cases. (*Wards Cove* case, cited in the bibliography).

42 U.S.C.§ 1981

As noted, 42 U.S.C. 1981 also affords protection against language discrimination on the job. That statute, as originally enacted following the Civil War, provides that:

all persons within the jurisdiction of the United States shall have the same right in every state and territory to make and enforce contracts, to sue, be parties, give evidence, and to the full and equal benefit of all laws and proceedings for the security of persons and property as is enjoyed by white citizens. . . .

Courts have interpreted this provision to protect against discriminatory hiring practices. Unlike the Equal Employment Opportunity Act cases, however, where a discrimination case can be made out generally by showing disparate impact upon a protected group, courts have found that a discrimination claim under 42 U.S.C. 1981 requires proof of discriminatory intent. Thus, where a Mr. Vasquez, who spoke only Spanish, had been periodically hired as a seasonal truck driver for the McAllen Bag and Supply Company in Texas and had performed his duties satisfactorily in the past, the refusal to rehire Mr. Vasquez after the company instituted a policy of hiring only English-speaking truck drivers was upheld. The court found that while the policy would tend to discriminate against Mexican-Americans because a significant number do not speak English, there was no showing that the employer who could communicate with his drivers only in English had the requisite discriminatory motive in instituting a policy of hiring only English-speaking or bilingual truck drivers.

One expert in employment discrimination law, Professor Player of the University of Georgia, has summarized the concerns relating to the hiring of only those people who can communicate in the English language as follows:

> Requiring that employees be able to communicate in the English language is not, on its face, national origin discrimination. However, the ability to speak and understand English obviously favors those of an Anglo heritage and disadvantages those who are reared in a non-Anglo environment. Notwithstanding this possible impact, the requirement can be justified as being 'necessary' at least to the extent that an English-speaking employer must be able to engage in essential communications with employees, and the employees among themselves.
>
> Making decisions based on a higher level of language ability presents a more difficult problem. It is clearly national

origin discrimination to impose on one ethnic group a language facility test not imposed on other groups. Even if the English test is imposed on all groups, given the adverse impact on particular ethnic groups, the employer can justify selecting employees on the basis of their relative ability with English only by proving the business necessity of the test. While a manual laborer can be required to know enough English to comprehend instructions and communicate with fellow workers, a test is not a business necessity if it measures an ability beyond that needed for communication. However, if the job requires a high level of English proficiency (for example, police officers, writers, teachers, sales personnel), it is permissible to utilize a test that measures more advanced language skills. (pp. 235, 236)

So far we have been concerned with a discussion of the right of an employer to limit employment to those people who speak only English and those who speak English with no accent. Given the recent dramatic increase in the Spanish-speaking population in this country, would an employer be justified in imposing a requirement that his or her employees demonstrate proficiency in Spanish or some other foreign language? If the language was a necessary part of the job, such as being able to serve as an interpreter (see Chapters 4 and 5) or responding to the requests of customers in another language, the imposition of foreign language proficiency would undoubtedly be upheld as a business necessity. (The U.S. Border Patrol requires that its officers be proficient in Spanish.) If, on the other hand, foreign language proficiency were used to exclude other racial or national origin groups without a showing of business necessity, the imposition would probably constitute impermissible discrimination.

It will be interesting to note if monolingual, English-speaking Americans suddenly become sensitized to the language rights issue if they find themselves denied employment opportunities because of a language barrier. In one recent case, a court upheld the validity of an employer's hiring requirement that employees be bilingual,

given the large Spanish-speaking clientele. Professor Player, on the other hand, seems to believe that while an
English-speaking employer could deny employment to
non-English-speaking applicants on the grounds they
could not communicate with him, he infers a non-English-
speaking employer would be required to hire an interpreter rather than deny employment to monolingual English speakers (Player, p. 236). This author suggests his
approach is incorrect, given the right of an employer to
require employees to be bilingual, and given the application of *Yu Cong Eng v. Trinidad*, a 1926 United States Supreme Court case discussed in Chapter 7 of this book. To
date no Spanish-only work rules have been the subject of
challenges in the courts.

Validity of English Only Rules at the Workplace

Just as rules prohibiting the hiring of people who do not
speak English very well or who speak English with a foreign accent run afoul of the prohibition against discrimination based on national origin in the absence of a business
necessity or a bona fide occupational qualification, so too
do blanket company rules prohibiting employees from
speaking a foreign language on the job. Administrative
decisions of the EEOC as far back as 1970 made clear the
proposition that an absolute prohibition against foreign
language communication among employees constitutes
national origin discrimination. Courts have also held that
broad English-only rules constitute unlawful discrimination. In one case decided in the United States District Court
for the Southern District of Texas in 1979, the court held
that unlawful employment discrimination had occurred
when a Mexican-American employee was discharged for
speaking two words of Spanish on the job, while another
employee was retained even though the second employee
was guilty of the more serious misdeed of engaging in a

fight during the same incident. The business in that case involved the drilling of a well. The court found that while the operation of a drilling rig is a highly skilled, dangerous operation requiring close coordination between members of the crew, and while ordinarily some limitation on the use of languages other than English might be appropriate for the business necessity of safety of personnel and of protection of property, the utterance of a casual Spanish phrase that caused no failure in communication and no danger could not form the basis of a discharge of the employee.

However, the scope of the right to language on the job was temporarily limited by the decision in a 1975 case entitled *Garcia v. Gloor.* Garcia was hired as a salesman by a lumber store in Brownsville, Texas. More than three-fourths of the population in the business area was Hispanic. Many of the store's customers expressed the desire to be waited on by Spanish-speaking salespeople. Garcia was hired precisely because he was bilingual. He was instructed to use English with English-speaking customers and Spanish with Spanish-speaking customers. However, the owner imposed another language rule on Garcia: even though three-fourths of the store's workers and customers spoke Spanish, Garcia and all other Spanish-speaking employees were forbidden from speaking Spanish on the job unless communicating with a Spanish-speaking customer. Among the reasons given by the owner for this rule was that the English-speaking customers (only one-fourth of the total population in the area) objected to the Spanish-speaking employees communicating among themselves in a language that the monolingual English customers did not understand. One day Garcia was asked a question by another Spanish-speaking clerk about an item requested by a customer. Garcia responded in Spanish that the article was not available. The owner overheard this exchange and fired Garcia. In rejecting Garcia's claim for relief under Title VII, the District Court found there were valid business reasons for the rule. On appeal, the Fifth Circuit Court upheld the District Court, refusing to critically examine either the validity of the business reasons offered or whether the business needs could be met in a less restrictive manner than the imposition of an English-only rule. The court found Garcia's conduct to be a deliberate violation of the rule, concluding that a language which a bilingual person elects to speak at a particular time is a matter of choice.

In 1987 the Ninth Circuit Court of Appeals upheld the termination of a disc jockey who claimed that the employer's English-only rule violated Title VII. The employer fired the announcer for speaking Spanish on the air in violation of the English-only work rule for broadcasting. The court concluded that there was a valid business necessity for the rule: a programming decision motivated by marketing, ratings, and demographic concerns.

However, current legal developments have cast serious doubt on the continuing validity of broad speak English work rules. In 1980 the Equal Employment Opportunity Commission adopted guidelines regarding such rules. The commission noted that rules requiring employees to speak only English at all times in the workplace is a burdensome term of employment. It noted that the primary language of an individual is often an essential national origin characteristic. It concluded that prohibiting employees at all times from speaking their primary language or the language they speak most comfortably, disadvantages an individual's employment opportunities on the basis of national origin. It may create an atmosphere of inferiority, isolation, and intimidation based on national origin, which could result in a discriminatory working environment. Therefore, the commission presumes, as a matter of law, that such a rule violates Title VII and will closely scrutinize it. Under the rules now in effect by the Equal Employment Opportunity Commission, an employer may have a rule requiring that an employee speak only in English at a certain time where the employer can show that the rule is justified by business necessity. However, the employer must inform its employees of the general circumstances when speaking only in English is required and of the consequences of violating the rule. The commission will consider the application of a speak-English-only rule as evidence of discrimination on the basis of national origin where an employer fails to effectively notify its employees and makes an adverse employment decision against an individual based on an alleged violation of the rule.

In a 1986 Houston Law Review article, this author also criticized the *Garcia v. Gloor* rationale, urging broader recognition of language rights in the workplace. The principles embodied in the EEOC regulations, the author's Houston Law Review article, and other sources were applied by the Ninth Circuit Court of Appeals in a 1988 case (*Gutierrez v. Mun. Ct.*), which expands the right of a worker to speak a language other than English on the job. An examination of this case is important, not only regarding the workplace issues, but later in a discussion of the applicability and validity of English-only statutes and constitutional provisions.

The plaintiff in that case, Alva Gutierrez, and a number of other bilingual Hispanic-Americans, were employed as deputy court clerks by the southeast judicial district of the Los Angeles Municipal Court. In March 1984 the Municipal Court, through its judges, enacted a new rule forbidding employees to speak any language other than English, except when acting as translators. The rule read:

> The English language shall be spoken by all court employees
> during regular working hours while attending to assigned
> work duties, unless an employee is translating for the non-
> English-speaking public. This rule does not apply to em-
> ployees while on their lunch hour or work breaks.

Ms. Gutierrez challenged the rule under Title VII using both adverse impact and disparate treatment theories. She also brought suit against the judges based on another post–Civil War civil rights statute, 42 U.S.C. § 1983. (This act prohibits persons, acting under color of state law, from violating the federally protected civil rights of another.) She contended that the rule, although allegedly facially neutral, unfairly disadvantages Hispanics because their ethnic identity is linked to the use of the Spanish language. She argued, alternatively, that the rule was intentionally adopted for the purpose of discriminating against Hispanics. She claimed that any neutral appearance was a mere pretext, and thus, the rule violates Title VII's prescription against disparate treatment as well.

In upholding an injunction against the rule, the Ninth Circuit Court of Appeals, citing sources including this author, found that the multicultural character of American society has a long and venerable history and is widely recognized as one of the United States' greatest strengths. It noted that while few courts have evaluated the lawfulness of workplace rules relating to the use of languages other than English, commentators generally agree that language is an important aspect of national origin. It noted, with approval, this author's conclusion that the primary language of an individual not only conveys certain concepts, but is itself an affirmation of that person's culture. It distinguished the *Jurado* case, noting that while an employer has a right to insist a broadcast be conducted exclusively in English because that is the product the employer was offering the public, the *Jurado* case did not involve an employer who was requiring employees to conduct off-the-air conversations in English.

The court had little difficulty disposing of the justifications offered by the municipal court judges for their English-only rule. The employer first asserted that because the United States is an English-speaking country, and California is an English-speaking state (as evidenced by its 1986 constitutional amendment making English the official language of the state), the municipal court would be justified in imposing English-only rules on its employees. The Ninth Circuit found this reason without merit. It noted that the prohibition of intraemployee Spanish communication does little to achieve English-speaking country and state status given that as part of their official duties, the court's bilingual employees are required to communicate in Spanish on a regular basis with numerous members of the non-English-speaking public. Next, the employers argued that the rule is necessary to prevent the workplace from turning into a Tower of Babel. The court concluded that allowing Spanish to be spoken is unlikely to create a much greater disruption than already exists, given that speaking in Spanish is necessary to the normal conducting of court business. Third, the Ninth Circuit had no trouble disposing of the employer's argument that the rule is necessary to promote racial harmony. It found this argument to be "generally unpersuasive," again citing this author, in noting that racial hostility increased among Hispanics and non-Spanish-speaking employees because Hispanics felt belittled by the English-only regulation. When the court considered the fourth argument of employers, that the English-only rule was necessary because several supervisors did not speak Spanish, the court concluded that the best way to ensure that supervisors are apprised of how well the bilingual employees are performing their task would be to employ Spanish-speaking supervisors. Finally, the court concluded that the California "official English" constitutional amendment does not create a business necessity.

The municipal court judges who lost the *Gutierrez* case before the three-judge panel sought to have the entire Ninth Circuit rehear the case. The request was denied, with one judge dissenting. They then sought review by the U.S. Supreme Court. In a one paragraph opinion, the Supreme Court found the case moot. Although the summary opinion does not identify why the court found the case to be moot, counsel for the municipal judges had urged in his briefs that the "English-only" rule had never gone into final effect, and that it would not be applicable to Ms. Gutierrez in any event because she no longer worked for the Municipal Court. He also urged that a monetary settlement paid by the County of Los Angeles to her made the case moot. Any or all of these reasons could have formed the basis for the Supreme Court ruling. In May 1989, the Ninth Circuit, upon order from the Supreme Court, vacated its opinion and dismissed the appeal. Nonetheless, the reasoning in the *Gutierrez* opinion of the Ninth Circuit's three-judge panel is still persuasive for other language rights cases which will undoubtedly follow.

The bottom line appears to be that employers may not terminate or discipline bilingual workers merely because those workers choose to speak Spanish or any other language to each other on the job. Even though the court in the *Garcia* case gave wide deference to the business owner, the owner had not attempted to impose an English-only rule on workers out in the yard, away from customers, nor during break times. Even the Fifth Circuit in 1975 would not have approved such a broad prohibition. Given that we now have the EEOC regulations and the *Gutierrez* case, an employer's limitation on the right of a worker to speak to a co-worker in the co-worker's language of choice will be upheld in only limited circumstances. Courts will probably now uphold speak English rules only upon a showing of a valid business reason including the safety and well-being of person and property in narrowly defined circumstances. An employer who wishes to impose such a rule is clearly going to need a valid reason for it. Employees will find a powerful ally in the courts on this issue.

Also, demographics and the marketplace may also be two important forces limiting the application of speak English rules. The increasing number of language minority workers in this country indicates that the language issue is not going to go away. This writer suggested in a 1986 article which appeared in the newsletter of the Kansas Advisory Committee on Hispanic Affairs that employees facing such a rule seek to discuss the matter in a nonhostile atmosphere with the employer. I noted that it is an unfortunate fact that many monolingual people often feel threatened by the use of a language they do not understand. An explanation, in a nonthreatening fashion, of the beauty of the language and the importance of its use by the worker, might go a long way towards alleviating some of the employer's misgivings. I went on to opine that the realization in 1986 of the growing impact of the Hispanic consumer in the marketplace might also mean that employers might be more flexible than was Mr. Garcia's employer in 1975. A recent survey seems to bear out the increase in Hispanic purchasing power. According to a November 1988 report by Telemundo, a new Spanish language television network in the United States, Hispanic consumers now spend $130 billion annually (1987), compared to $80 billion in 1983.

A study conducted in 1988 by Professor David L. Gregory of St. John's University Law School also confirms that demographics will play an important role in limiting the application of future English-only rules in the workplace:

> Given the labor shortage already severely afflicting some employers, and projected to become more exacerbated in the coming decade, the pristine niceties of case law may soon become quite academic. Rather than seek to refine rigid 'English only' work rules ad infinitum, even the most parochial employers may be pragmatically forced by changing workforce demographics to not only tolerate, but affirmatively to seek out, multilingual and multicultural employees in order to staff operations with sufficient personnel. Fortunately, the 'English only' work rule cases are now destined for quick obsolescence by labor shortages and rapidly changing workplace demographics, and need not await the evolution of a more sensitive jurisprudence.

Right to Union Participation

Up to this point in this chapter we have been primarily concerned with the relationship between employer and employee in the context of language issues on the job. Another series of statutes and cases deal with the right of an employee who does not happen to speak English to be represented by a union and participate in its activities. The seminal work in this area is an article by Professor Gregory entitled *Union Leadership and Workers' Voices: Meeting the Needs of Linguistically Heterogeneous Union Members.* That article explores these issues in detail, and should be consulted by anyone with a further interest in this topic. In very brief summary form, however, we will attempt to summarize some of the major legal precedents in this area.

The National Labor Relations Act is an extensive regulatory act which seeks to regulate labor relations in activities affecting interstate and foreign commerce. One major purpose of the act is to protect interstate commerce by securing to employees the rights established in Section 7 of the act to organize, bargain collectively through representatives of their own choosing, and to engage in concerted activities for that, and other purposes. It seeks to open the way for collective bargaining on a basis of equality of bargaining power between employers and freely chosen representatives of employees. The National Labor Relations Board is given the exclusive initial power under the act to determine whether it has jurisdiction over a particular employer in labor-related matters. It also has supervisory authority over elections to determine whether a particular labor union will be entitled to represent a group of employees. The worker who does not speak English would obviously face a serious obstacle in participating in a union representation election if the voting materials were only made available in English. Accordingly, even though nothing in the National Labor Relations Act specifically requires multilingual election notices and ballots, the National Labor Relations Board has found that non-English-speaking bargaining unit members must be provided with bilingual election notices in order for them to make sufficient and informed decisions. Courts, particularly the Fifth Circuit Court of Appeals, have imposed an even higher standard, requiring that not only the notice of the election but also the actual ballots must be printed in languages understood by language minority workers. An important limitation upon this right, however, is, as Professor Gregory notes,

"The Board will set aside an election only if the challenging party could show the lack of bilingual materials had a markedly adverse, outcome determinative impact upon the ability of employees to cast an informed vote."

Assuming that a fair election has been held and a union has been selected to represent workers in a particular bargaining unit, another series of questions revolves around the duty of the union at that point to provide translation of the collective bargaining agreement and bilingual meetings in order to allow the language minority workers to be represented by the union and participate in its activities. In an important 1987 case, the Ninth Circuit considered the validity of an English-only rule enacted by a union which provided that union meetings would be conducted only in the English language. A Spanish-speaking member of the union who did not understand English brought suit against the union alleging that the rule violated portions of the Landman Griffith Act of 1959, the Labor Management Reporting and Disclosure Act, 29 U.S.C. § 411(a)(1). The court held the English-only rule to be a violation of the equal participation rights guaranteed by the statute. It ordered the union to provide independent translators to translate all debate and shop talk at monthly membership meetings. The majority concluded that the translation would be necessary to allow equal opportunity for all union members given that 48 percent of the members of the union spoke only Spanish. Professor Gregory has concluded, in another variation on this theme, that so far only one case at the federal court of appeals level has suggested that union failure to provide translation of the collective bargaining agreement and bilingual union representatives may breach the union's duty of fair representation to those employees.

Again, even though there is a limited framework for the protection of the rights of the language minority workers vis-a-vis his or her union, Professor Gregory notes the encouraging trend among some unions, given the rising importance of foreign language workers, to institute lan-

guage skills training programs while affording interpretation and translation to overcome difficulties caused by language barriers.

Employment discrimination issues in a language context
are procedurally complex. The conflicting jurisdiction of
federal and state statutes, and human rights bodies in
counties, municipalities, or in larger institutions, make the
presentation of such claims all the more complicated.
Moreover, the impact of two employment discrimination
cases decided by the U.S. Supreme Court as this book was
being finalized in June 1989 will undoubtedly be the subject
of further litigation and scholarly debate. In one, *Wards
Cove*, the Court relaxed the employer's burden of proof in
disparate impact cases. In the other, the *Patterson* case, the
Court determined that 42 U.S.C. §1981 covers conduct at
the initial formation of an employment contract, but does
not reach postformation racial harassment in employment.
Despite these complications, judicial and administrative
remedies remain very much available for language discrimination cases.

Yet another issue arises: If a person with limited English
ability has a right to proceed with a language discrimination grievance in court or before an administrative agency,
how can that person obtain relief if the agency or court only
conducts its business in English? For a somewhat complicated answer, we turn now to a discussion of the availability of interpretation assistance in courts (Chapter 4) and
before administrative bodies (Chapter 5).

Bibliography

Books

M. Player, *Employment Discrimination Law* (1988).
48 Am.Jur.2d, *Labor* (1979).

Articles

1. Davis, *Garcia v. Gloor: Mutable Characteristics Rationale Extended to National Origin Discrimination*, 32 Mercer L. Rev. 1275 (1981).
2. Gregory, *Union Leadership and Workers' Voices: Meeting the Needs of Linguistically Heterogeneous Union Members*, 58 Cinc. L. Rev. __ (July, 1989).
3. Karst, Paths to Belonging: *The Constitution and Cultural Identity*, 64 N.C.L. Rev. 303 (1986).
4. Piatt, *Spanish on the Job: Business Needs and Employee Rights*, "La Voz del Llano," Kansas Advisory Committee on Hispanic Affairs, Vol. 5 No. 4 (July, 1986).
5. Note, *Language Discrimination Under Title VII: The Silent Right of National Origin Discrimination*, 15 J. Marshall L. Rev. 667 (1982).
6. Note, *National Origin Discrimination Under Section 1981*, 51 Fordham L. Rev. 919 (1983).

Federal Statutes, Regulations

1. Title VII, Civil Rights Act of 1964 ("Equal Employment Opportunity Act"), 42 U.S.C. § 2000e (1981).
2. Civil Rights Act of 1866, now 42 U.S.C. § 1981 (1981).
3. Act of April 20, 1871, now 42 U.S.C. § 1983 (1981).
4. 29 C.F.R. § 1606.7: "Speak-English-Only Rules" (1988).

Labor Statutes (all located in 29 U.S.C.):

National Labor Relations Act of 1935 (also known as the "Wagner Act").

Labor-Management Relations Act of 1947 (also known as the Taft-Hartley Act).

Labor Management Reporting and Disclosure Act of 1959 (also known as the Landrum-Griffin Act).

Selected Federal Judicial Administrative Decisions

1. *Carino v. University of Okla. Bd. of Regents,* 750 F.2d 815 (10th Cir. 1984).
2. *Fragante v. City and County of Honolulu,* __ F.2nd __, 57 U.S.L.W. 2557 (4/4/89).
3. *Garcia v. Gloor,* 618 F.2d 264 (5th Cir. 1980).
4. *Gutierrez v. Municipal Court,* 838 F.2d 1031 (9th Cir. 1988), vacated as moot, 57 U.S.L.W. 3687 (4/18/89).
5. *Jones v. United Gas Imp. Corp.,* 68 F.R.D. 1 (E.D. Pa. 1975).
6. *Jurado v. Eleven-Fifty Corp.,* 813 F.2d 1406 (9th Cir. 1988).
7. *Patterson v. McLean Credit Union,* 109 S.Ct. 2363 (1989).
8. *Saucedo v. Brothers Well Serv., Inc.,* 464 F. Supp. 919 (S.D. Tex. 1979).
9. *Smith v. District of Columbia,* 29 F.E.P. 1129 (D.D.C. 1982).
10. *Retana v. Apartment Operators Local 14,* 453 F.2d 1018 (9th Cir. 1972).
11. *Vasquez v. McAllen Bag & Supply Co.,* 660 F.2d 686 (5th Cir. 1981).
12. *Wards Cove Packing Co. Inc. v. Antonio,* 109 S.Ct. 2115 (1989).
13. *Zamora v. Local 11,* 817 F.2d 566 (9th Cir. 1987).
14. 2 Fair Empl. Prac. Cas. (BNA) No. YAU 9–048 at 78 (June 30, 1969).
15. 1973 EEOC Decisions (CCH) No. 71–446 ¶ 6173 (Nov. 5, 1970).

Chapter 4

Courtroom Interpreters

On several occasions I have introduced the topic of the right to a courtroom interpreter by discussing an incident that occurred during my first semester of law school at the University of New Mexico. The District Court Clerk's office called the school looking for an interpreter. A criminal trial was in progress and a witness could only speak Spanish. Would a bilingual law student be interested in assisting, the Clerk's office asked? Out of a sense of civic duty and with the incentive of earning some badly needed money, a friend volunteered. He rushed to court, stood before the judge and jury, and was asked to inquire of the witness: "Do you solemnly swear or affirm under penalty of perjury that the testimony you are about to give will be the truth, the whole truth, and nothing but the truth?" My friend was intelligent, conversant in Spanish, and well-educated. However, the pressure of the stares from the judge and jury and the legal terminology caused his mind to draw a blank. He turned to the witness, and in Spanish inquired: "You're not going to lie, are you?" My friend and I learned from that experience what formal studies would later prove: It is a mistake to believe that a person can serve as an interpreter just because he or she is bilingual; language misunderstandings in the courtroom can have potentially disastrous effects on the rights of parties and witnesses. In this chapter we explore the sources and parameters of the right to language interpretation in the courtroom.

Constitutional Basis for a Right to an Interpreter

The United States Supreme Court has never clearly defined the constitutional basis for a right to an interpreter in either criminal or civil trials.

Through the middle of the twentieth century, it was generally held that the appointment of courtroom interpreters in criminal proceedings would be a matter resting solely in the trial court's discretion. In civil cases, where litigants could afford their own interpreters, courts often permitted their use, but did not and still do not find any constitutional basis for having a court appoint and pay for an interpreter in such cases.

Even after provisions were enacted allowing the appointment of interpreters in criminal proceedings in the federal courts, an appointment was still considered to be a matter of discretion with the trial court. No constitutional right to a free simultaneous translator was inferred from the apparent power of the court to make such an appointment.

However, in 1970, the Second Circuit Court of Appeals announced a clear constitutional basis for the right to an interpreter in a criminal proceeding in a case entitled *U.S. ex rel. Negron v. New York*. In that case, Mr. Negron, a twenty-three-year-old indigent with a sixth grade Puerto Rican education who neither spoke nor understood any English, was charged with murder. His court-appointed lawyer spoke no Spanish. During the trial, the testimony of Mr. Negron in Spanish and that of two other Spanish-speaking witnesses was translated into English by an interpreter for the benefit of the judge, the prosecution, and the

jury. That interpreter met briefly with Negron and his attorney during two brief recesses in the course of a four-day
trial. However, the interpreter never translated English
language testimony into Spanish for Negron while the trial
was in progress. Mr. Negron was convicted of murder and
appealed. He claimed that he had been denied his right, as
guaranteed by the Sixth Amendment to the United States
Constitution, to "be confronted with the witnesses against
him" in his criminal prosecution. The Second Circuit Court
of Appeals agreed with him and reversed his conviction. It
determined that this confrontation clause, made applicable
to the states through the Fourteenth Amendment's Due
Process Clause (refer to Chapter 2 for a discussion of this
incorporation process), requires that non-English-speaking defendants be informed of their right to simultaneous
interpretation of proceedings at the government's expense.
Otherwise, the trial would be a "babble of voices." The
defendant would not understand the testimony against
him. Defendant's attorney would be hampered in effective
cross-examination of the witnesses against his or her client.
The court went on to note:

> Not only for the sake of effective cross-examination, how-
> ever, but as a matter of simple humaneness, Negron de-
> served more than to sit in total incomprehension as the trial
> proceeded. Particularly inappropriate in this nation where
> many languages are spoken is a callousness to the crippling
> language handicap of a newcomer to its shores, whose life
> and freedom the state by its criminal processes chooses to
> put in jeopardy.

Courts have repeatedly determined that there is no constitutional right to an interpreter in a civil proceeding, nor
in administrative matters. After all, the Sixth Amendment
only applies to criminal prosecutions. (In Chapters 5 and
10, however, we take up the issue as to whether or not due
process should require the appointment of interpreters in
these cases as well.) Even though the United States Supreme Court has not spoken definitively on the issue,

lower court decisions have established beyond reasonable argument that there is a constitutional basis for a right to an interpreter in a criminal prosecution, although occasionally a court will erroneously hold otherwise. Beyond a constitutional basis, various statutes and court rule provisions provide for interpreters. We will examine some of those statutes and rules in the next section.

Statutory Basis for Interpreters

With *Negron* serving as the impetus, the right to an interpreter in the federal courts was expanded by enactment by the United States Congress of the Court Interpreters Act in 1978. The act requires judges to utilize competent interpreters in criminal or civil actions initiated by the United States in a United States district court. An interpreter must be appointed when a party or witness speaks only or primarily in a language other than English, or suffers from a hearing impairment so as to inhibit the person's comprehension of the proceedings, communication with counsel or the judge, or so as to inhibit the witness's comprehension of questions in the presentation of testimony. The Director of the Administrative Office of the United States Courts is required to prescribe, determine, and certify the qualifications of persons who may serve as interpreters. The director maintains a list of interpreters and prescribes a fee schedule for their use. A serious limitation on the right to an interpreter in the federal courts under this act is that the right only exists in cases that are brought by the United States government.

Many state statutes, on the other hand, provide for a much broader right to an interpreter in state courts. A Kansas statute, for example, requires that qualified interpreters be appointed for persons whose primary language is other than English, or who are deaf or mute. Under this law, interpreters must be appointed for parties or witnesses before grand juries, or in any court proceeding where the person with the language, hearing, or speech impairment faces confinement or penal sanctions. The right also applies in any civil proceeding, and not just those brought by the government. The right to an interpreter exists in administrative hearings or even when the person is arrested for criminal or city ordinance violations. Other states, through statutes and rules, also provide for potentially broader right to an interpreter than under the federal act. A listing of several state statutes dealing with interpreters is included in the bibliography. There are also discretionary provisions in the rules of procedure in many states which give a court the power to appoint interpreters in appropriate cases.

Even though *Negron,* the Court Interpreters Act, and state authorities now leave little doubt that there are constitutional and statutory rights to courtroom interpreters, the determination as to whether a particular applicant is entitled to the appointment and the manner of proceeding through the use of an interpreter is still committed to the trial court's discretion. We turn now to examining how courts exercise this discretion in affording the right to a courtroom interpreter.

Who Is Entitled to an Interpreter?

The first thought that may come to mind in response to this question, is that it is obvious whether or not a person speaks English. Applying this gut level standard, courts sometimes determine, in the exercise of their discretion, that a person or witness who speaks some English is not entitled to an interpreter. In a 1986 Nebraska case, *State v. Topete,* it was held that the trial court did not abuse its discretion in failing to appoint an interpreter for a defendant who had conversed with an officer and a jailer in English. In other cases, where judges or witnesses overhear the person engage in social conversations in English, the courts have held there is no right to an interpreter.

However, proficiency in a language, like other skills, is a matter of degree. For example, many people who would insist that they do not know the Spanish language would readily acknowledge that they understand the meaning of *adios*, *taco*, and many other Spanish words. They could successfully guess at the meaning of *gasolina* and *restaurante*. Similarly, any person who speaks a language other than English who spends more than twenty-four hours in this country is almost certain to pick up some English vocabulary. Those foreign language immigrants who have spent a considerable amount of time here probably will have acquired even greater skills, perhaps even the ability to carry on social conservation. This ability to communicate socially in English, however, should not be confused with an ability to sufficiently understand the proceedings in a court of law to communicate effectively as a witness or with counsel. A study conducted on behalf of the Director of the Administrative Office of the United States Courts pursuant to the Court Interpreters Act found that because of the sophisticated language level used in the courts, it is necessary to have a minimum of fourteen years of education to understand what goes on in a criminal trial and more than that in a civil trial. As a result, the person who can only converse socially in English is going to be lost in such a proceeding without an interpreter. In fact, the statutory test under the Court Interpreters Act and the majority view among state statutes is that an interpreter must be appointed when a party or witness speaks only or primarily in a language other than English, or suffers from a hearing impairment, so as to inhibit the person's comprehension of the proceedings, communication with counsel or the judge, or so as to inhibit the witness's comprehension of questions in the presentation of testimony. Under this test, the person who demonstrates some limited ability to socially converse in English could not legally be denied an interpreter, at least not in a proceeding covered by *Negron*, the Court Interpreters Act, or a similar state statute.

Who Is Qualified to Serve as an Interpreter?

Even assuming that a court is convinced that a person has the right to an interpreter, another legal issue which must be resolved is a determination as to who is qualified to serve as the interpreter. In the federal system, the Director of the Administrative Office of the federal courts examines and certifies interpreters. Some states maintain similar listings. In the absence of such certification, however, the trial judge must be satisfied that the interpreter demonstrates sufficient education, training, and experience to make a competent translation. This test is important, because even where a certified interpreter is required, the law provides that where none is available, the trial judge may go ahead and appoint a competent, although uncertified, interpreter. (See the New Mexico statute listed in the bibliography.) It is important to recognize that a competent interpreter must be fluent in both English and the foreign language.

Often a problem arises because of a lack of certified or otherwise competent interpreters. In those circumstances, although a judge is ordinarily required to hear any issues regarding interpreter bias, courts have routinely held that an interpreter need not be the least interested person available in order to quality for appointment. Thus, courts have taken the position that it is not error per se for a court to select a close friend or relative of a witness to serve as his or her interpreter. Some cases even permit biased interpreters. In one instance in Texas, an assistant district attorney was allowed to serve as an interpreter for a prosecution witness. In a New Jersey case, the mother of a four-year-old victim of a crime was allowed to serve as an interpreter for her son to interpret his words and gestures. In what this author and several courts view as a serious conflict-of-interest problem, bilingual attorneys have even been required to serve as interpreters for their own clients. And in perhaps an even more bizarre situation, the presence of a trial judge who speaks the native language of the person who ordinarily would be entitled to an interpreter has been held to negate the right of the language minority client to a court-appointed translator.

How Is the Right to an Interpreter Most Effectively Implemented in the Courtroom?

Trials are conducted with attorneys asking questions of witnesses and introducing documents and other items into evidence for consideration by a judge, or in some cases, a jury. A court reporter takes down the exact words of the attorney and the witness through various means. If there is an appeal of the case, the court reporter then prepares a typed transcript listing the questions and the answers, the comments and rulings of the judge, and the other matters which occurred at trial. The matter becomes somewhat more complicated with the presence of questioning through an interpreter. The trial judge must make several decisions, even after he or she rules that a person is entitled to an interpreter and decides on someone qualified and competent to serve as an interpreter. Among these decisions is whether the person entitled to an interpreter will be afforded a literal translation as opposed to a mere summary of the witness's testimony. In several cases it has been held that the right to an interpreter does not guarantee the right to a literal translation. The better view is that expressed in *Negron* where witness summaries were disapproved, and the right to a literal, simultaneous translation was upheld. A first-person translation will also make the record more intelligible. Perhaps an illustration would help at this point.

As noted, the court reporter will take down the questions of the attorney and the responses, in English. In the ordinary case, where there is no language barrier nor an interpreter, an excerpt from a transcript might look like this:

1. Attorney (in English   'What is your
   to witness):   name?'
2. Witness (in English):   'My name is John
     Doe.'   (example #1)

Where an interpreter is present, and where the judge is affording a simultaneous, first-person translation, the following exchange would occur:

1. Attorney (in English):   'What is your
     name?'
2. Interpreter (in   'What is your
   foreign language   name?'
   to witness):
3. Witness (in foreign   'My name is John
   language):   Doe.'
4. Interpreter (in   'My name is John
   English):   Doe.'   (example #2)

Even though the words in lines 1, 2, 3, and 4 would have been spoken in the courtroom, the court reporter would only transcribe the English dialogue. As a result, the only information that would appear in the record would be lines 1 and 4, which is the same question and answer that would have appeared where there was no need for an interpreter (compare with example #1 above). Use of the simultaneous translation allows the attorneys and the parties in the court to contemporaneously understand the testimony. It allows attorneys to make any objections they are required to make. Use of the first-person by the interpreter (and second person by the attorney) creates a more intelligible record than if the interpreter responds, for example, "He says his name is John Doe." In the simple example (example # 2), no great confusion would occur even if the interpreter had responded in the third person. In more complicated exchanges, however, the record could become garbled if the interpreter translates in the third person:

Question: Ask him who was there.
Answer: He says his friends, Juan and Fred.

Question: Ask him if he signed the paper.
Answer: He said they did.
Question: Who did?
Answer: He said him and Juan.   (example #3)

We are not sure, for example, sitting in the courtroom or reading the record later to whom "he and him" refer. (A New Mexico Court Reporter, Mr. Howard Henry, urges the use of first person to avoid confusion in this situation.)

Another issue facing the courts in the use of interpreters is a decision whether to require the presence of two interpreters. This author has frequently used the following (admittedly absurd) example to demonstrate why, without the presence of two interpreters, an interpretation error could be made without anyone in the courtroom even being aware an error had occurred:

1. Attorney (in English):   'What is your name?'
2. Interpreter (in foreign   'What did you eat for
   language to witness):   breakfast?'
3. Witness (in foreign   'Ham and eggs.'
   language):
4. Interpreter (in English):   'My name is John Doe.'

Obviously there is no third-person or simultaneous translation problem with this interpretation. The problem is a misinterpretation. If all attorneys and parties only speak English and if the witness only speaks the foreign language, the only person in the room who knows there has been an error made is the interpreter. If the interpreter does not intentionally make the error, but rather makes the error for a lack of precision in one or both languages, nobody will catch the error. The record will only contain lines 1 and 4, which is not an accurate reflection of the witness's testimony. Accordingly, to protect the interest of a client who speaks no English, an attorney should have his or her own interpreter in addition to the court interpreter. The interpreter sitting with counsel would immediately notify counsel of the translation error. Counsel could object, and call the second interpreter as a witness to testify regarding the translation error, if need be. (If the attorney were bilingual, he or she would catch the error without the second interpreter, but attorneys' ethics would prohibit that attorney from both testifying on behalf of the client and continuing as counsel.) Courts have in fact appointed two interpreters in appropriate cases.

Another reason why two interpreters are often necessary relates to the need of the client to consult with monolingual counsel. Consider the scenario where an English-speaking attorney represents a Spanish-speaking client in a criminal trial. The prosecution witness testifies in Spanish. An interpreter translates into English for benefit of court and counsel, thereby enabling defendant, through counsel, to confront the witness by means of cross-examination. However, defendant could not point out inaccuracies in the testimony to defense counsel without either halting the proceedings and having the interpreter approach the counsel table, or waiting until the end of the witness's testimony when memory has faded or the time for objection had passed. In any event, there might exist potential damage to the client's right to maintain confidential communication with defense counsel, particularly if the interpreter were a prosecuting attorney, police officer, or friend or relative of the victim.

These matters relating to the use of interpreters at trial are admittedly somewhat technical. If the reader can stand a brief discussion of another technical aspect of the use of courtroom interpreters, it is this. Attorneys for clients with limited English ability who are using interpreters should insist that the testimony be tape-recorded for correcting errors at trial or for transmission with the record on appeal if necessary. After all, in an appeal, the appellate court will only read the words on the transcript and will not have the opportunity to listen to the witnesses. In at least one case, *Pham*, the tape recording was used as a mechanism of preserving the error that an interpreter might make, for review by an appellate court. Amendments to the Court

Interpreters Act in 1988 require recording of interpreted grand jury testimony upon motion of the defendant, and permit a federal court to record other testimony when interpreters are used.

So far in this chapter we have discussed exclusively the interpretation process in the courtroom once a trial has begun. However, courts have intervened on behalf of persons with limited English ability where that language barrier would have precluded the person from even getting to court in the first place. A brief discussion of these cases follows.

Verified Complaints

A civil lawsuit is ordinarily initiated with the filing of a complaint or petition. Ordinarily, the complaint is signed by the plaintiff's attorney, and a copy is served upon the defendant. In some instances, the law requires that the complaint be verified by the plaintiff. That means that the plaintiff must swear, under penalties of perjury, that all of the statements and allegations in the complaint are true.

In 1966 the Supreme Court of the United States had occasion to consider the application of this requirement to a language minority plaintiff in the case of *Surowitz v. Hilton Hotels Corporation.* Mrs. Surowitz was a Polish immigrant with a very limited English vocabulary and practically no formal education. For many years she worked as a seamstress in New York City where, by reason of her frugality, she saved enough money to buy some stock in the Hilton Hotels Corporation. Her son-in-law, a Harvard Law School graduate with a master's degree in economics from Columbia University and a professional investment advisor, determined that a fraudulent scheme was being engaged in by the officers and directors of the corporation. He counseled Mrs. Surowitz to bring a lawsuit. The type of lawsuit that she filed, a shareholder's derivative action, requires that the complaint be verified. Mrs. Surowitz signed an

English language complaint and the verification. The defendants succeeded in having the lower courts throw out her complaint, upon a showing that she, because of her lack of education and limited language ability, really did not understand the words in the complaint. She did, however, understand what her son-in-law had told her about the case. On appeal the United States Supreme Court reversed the lower courts and reinstated Mrs. Surowitz's lawsuit. The Court concluded,

> If rules of procedure work as they should in an honest and fair judicial system, they not only permit, but should as nearly as possible guarantee that bona fide complaints be carried to an adjudication on the mertis.

Default Judgments

Once a complaint in a civil case is filed with the court and a copy served upon the defendant, the defendant has a relatively short period of time (usually twenty or thirty days) in which to file a formal answer. If the defendant does not file a formal answer, a default judgment can be entered against him or her. This means that the defendant loses without a trial. What happens if, because of a language barrier, a person is unable to understand and respond to the allegations in the English language complaint?

Ordinarily, ignorance of the English language is not an excuse for failing to respond to a lawsuit, at least where the person knows that he or she is being sued. However, where the person does not, because of the language barrier, even understand the nature of the proceedings, courts have invalidated the default judgment obtained against such a person. A good example of this principle is a 1972 decision of an Arizona appellate court in the case of *Cota v. Southern Arizona Bank & Trust Co.* There, a father with limited English language ability signed a note guaranteeing payment on his son's auto loan, after a bank official told him his son would be thrown in jail if the father did not sign. (Such a failing would have been unlawful—one may not be lawfully jailed for debt in this country.) The son failed to make payments and the bank sued the father. The father mistakenly believed the summons and complaint were merely a notice to make payments faster. In fact, he then went to the bank and made a payment which the bank accepted. The bank obtained a default judgment against the father. On appeal, the judgment was set aside because of the language barrier. The court allowed the father to proceed with his defense of duress. The father apparently was effectively coerced into signing the loan by the unlawful threats of the bank, and that, if proven, would constitute a defense to his having to pay off the loan.

Several final comments are important before closing this discussion of courtroom interpreters. The first is that while the emphasis of this chapter and this book is on language issues, the interpretation principles in the courtroom setting apply equally to hearing or speech-impaired litigants or witnesses. The importance of interpretation issues for the hearing or speech-impaired was underlined in a 1925 Alabama case, *Terry v. State:* "The physical infirmity of this appellant (a deaf-mute for whom no interpreter was provided at trial) can in no sense lessen his rights under the Constitution."

Second, the need for interpreters, particularly Spanish language interpreters, is growing. According to a study conducted by the Administrative Office of the U.S. Courts, which became part of the legislative history of the Court Interpreter Amendments Act of 1988, interpreted proceedings constituted six percent of all federal court proceedings in 1986. Proceedings requiring languages other than Spanish constituted only one-third of one percent of all federal court actions. In all, certified Spanish language interpreters were used 33,764 times in the U.S. district courts in 1986. Yet few persons can interpret with the level of precision required by the federal courts. The administrative office as of 1986 had spent over $1,000,000 in test development and administration, had given the Spanish interpretation test more than 7,000 times (some have taken it more than once), and yet had been able to certify only 292 interpreters.

Third, while the procedural aspects involved in litigation make the discussion of courtroom interpreters seem somewhat technical and perhaps abstract, these issues are often critical. For a dramatic portrayal of injustice and death resulting from a language misinterpretation, the reader is referred to the 1982 movie *The Ballad of Gregorio Cortez,* based upon the book *With His Pistol in His Hand: A Border Ballad and Its Hero,* both of which are cited in the bibliography.

Bibliography

Book

Paredes, *With His Pistol in his Hand: A Border Ballad and Its Hero* (1971).

Articles

1. Annotation, *Disqualification, for Bias, of One Offered as Interpreter of Testimony,* 6 A.L.R. 4th 158 (1981).
2. Annotation, *Right of Accused to Have Evidence or Court Proceedings Interpreted,* 36 A.L.R. 3d 276 (1971).
3. Chang & Araujo, *Interpreters for the Defense: Due Process for the Non–English-Speaking Defendant,* 63 Calif. L. Rev. 801 (1975).
4. Grabau and Williamson, *Language Barriers in Our Trial Courts: The Use of Court Interpreters in Massachusetts,* 70 Mass. L. Rev. 108 (1985).
5. Henry, *On the Record,* N.M. Bar Bull., Feb. 17, 1983, special insert at 1.

6. Piatt, *A Matter of Interpretation,* "The Circuit Rider," Washburn Law School Assoc., Vol. 23, No. 3, Summer 1984.
7. Piatt, *Attorney as Interpreter: A Return to Babble,* 20 N.M. L. Rev. ——— (1989).
8. Comment, *Trying Non-English Conversant Defendants: The Use of an Interpreter,* 57 Or. L. Rev. 549 (1978).
9. Note, *The Right to an Interpreter,* 25 Rutgers L. Rev. 145 (1970).

Federal Constitutional Provisions, Statutes

U.S. Const. amend. VI.
U.S. Const. amend. XIV.
Court Interpreters Act, 28 U.S.C. § 1827 (1988).
Court Interpreters Amendments Act of 1988, Pub. L. No. 100–702, 102 Stat. 4654 (1988).

"Discretionary" Provisions

1. 18 U.S.C. § 3006A(e) (1985, as amended 1987).
2. Fed. R. Civ. P. 43(f) (1968, as amended 1987).
3. Fed. R. Crim. P. 28 (1975).
4. Fed. R. Evid. 604.

Selected Federal Judicial Decisions

1. *Cervantes v. Cox,* 350 F.2d 855 (10th Cir. 1965) (Spanish-speaking defendant has no right to Spanish-speaking attorney).
2. *Guerrero v. Harris,* 461 F. Supp. 583 (S.D.N.Y. 1978) (no interpreter where defendant conversed in English).
3. *Perovich v. United States,* 205 U.S. 86 (1907) (appointment of interpreter discretionary).
4. *Seltzer v. Foley,* 502 F. Supp. 600 (S.D.N.Y. 1980) (study re: sophisticated language level in courts).
5. *Surowitz v. Hilton Hotels Corp.,* 383 U.S. 363 (1966).
6. *United States v. Desist,* 384 F.2d 889 (2d Cir. 1967) (no interpreter where judge spoke language of defendant).

7. *United States ex rel Negron v. New York,* 434 F.2d 386 (2d Cir. 1970).

Selected State Interpreter Provisions

1. Cal. Const. art. I, § 14.
2. Fla. Stat. Ann. § 90.606 (West 1985).
3. Iowa Code Ann. § 622A (West 1988).
4. Kan. Stat. Ann. § 75–4351 (1984).
5. Mass. Gen. Laws Ann. ch. 221C (West 1988).
6. Neb. Rev. Stat. art. 24 (1985).
7. N.J. Stat. Ann., § 2A:11–28 (West 1987).
8. N.M. Stat. Ann. § 38–10–1 (1978).
9. Tex. Crim. Proc. Code Ann. art. 38.30 (Vernon's 1988).
10. Wash. Rev. Code Ann. ch. 2.42 (1988).

Selected State Judicial Decisions

1. *COTA v. Southern Ariz. Bank & Trust Co.,* 17 Ariz. App. 326, 497 P.2d 833 (1972).
2. *Jara v. Municipal Court,* 21 Cal. 3d 181, 578 P.2d 94, 145 Cal. Rptr. 847 (1978) (no constitutional right to court-appointed interpreter in civil cases).
3. *People v. Estrada,* 176 Cal. App. 3d 410, 221 Cal. Rptr. 922 (1986) (implicit recognition of right to *two* interpreters; see also St. v. Pham).
4. *State v. Pham,* 234 Kan. 649, 675 P.2d 848 (1984) (use of interpreters in Kansas).
5. *State v. Rios,* 112 Ariz. 143, 539 P.2d 900 (1975) (bilingual attorney cannot serve as client's interpreter).
6. *State v. Topete,* 221 Neb. 771, 380 N.W.2d 635 (1986) (no interpreter where defendant conversed in jail in English).
7. *Terry v. State,* 21 Ala. App. 100, 105 So. 386 (1925).

Other

The Ballad of Gregorio Cortez (Moctesuma Productions, Inc., 1982).
Legislative History, Court Interpreter Amendments Act of 1988, 1989 U.S. Code Cong. & Admin. News, p. 6018 et seq.

Chapter 5

Social Service Agencies

In Chapter 4 we discussed the right to an interpreter in a courtroom setting. Language assistance is very important in administrative settings outside of the courtroom as well. Indeed, the relative interests involved in many administrative proceedings may be even more pressing than in the courtroom. Consider, for example, the impact upon poor families of the loss of public assistance. Many would conclude that such a termination would carry a potentially devastating impact, especially regarding children, with much more serious consequences involved than in a relatively minor criminal proceeding.

Nonetheless, courts have been reluctant up to this point to identify a constitutional basis for a right to an interpreter before social service agencies. Spanish-speaking welfare recipients, for example, were held to have no constitutional right to be notified in Spanish of the termination or reduction of their benefits. At the administrative hearing where the loss of the benefits would be an issue, it has been held that there would be no constitutional right to an interpreter. Ironically, however, in deportation proceedings where the issue is the loss of the right to remain in this country, undocumented persons are held to have a constitutional right to an interpreter before the Immigration and Naturalization Service.

Important legislative exceptions to the general rule, however, have been carved out. Some states, such as Kansas, affirmatively provide for interpretive assistance in administrative matters. Further, courts have concluded that under a national origin theory, federal statutes and regulations provide some protection to language minority individuals seeking assistance through federally funded programs. We examine these conflicting policies in this chapter.

Courts Find No Constitutional Basis for Administrative Interpretation.

One leading case in this area is a 1973 California Supreme Court case entitled *Guerrero v. Carlson*. The plaintiffs were three individuals who had been receiving Aid to Families with Dependent Children (AFDC), which is an assistance program funded by federal, state, and local governments. (The program, incidentally, is commonly referred to as being part of the welfare system.) The plaintiffs were Spanish speakers who did not communicate in English. Under applicable regulations, recipients of such assistance are entitled to receive timely and adequate notice of any proposed reduction or termination of benefits. *Adequate* means, pursuant to the regulations, that the notice must include a written explanation of the reasons for the proposed action, of the recipients' right to request a fair hearing, and of the fact that benefits will continue to be paid throughout the hearing period if the request for hearing is made within fifteen days (the *timely* provision). In the *Guerrero* case, the state of California sent notices of reduction or termination of benefits to the plaintiffs in the English language. When the plaintiffs failed, because they did not understand the material, to request a fair hearing within the fifteen-day period, their benefits were terminated. The plaintiffs filed suit. They alleged, and the defendants agreed, that the welfare authorities knew that the individual plaintiffs in this case did not speak or read English. The California lower courts refused to give the plaintiffs the right to a hearing and the California Supreme Court held that notice was not constitutionally required to be given in Spanish or in any other foreign language. The opinion of the court based its decision in part upon the fact that "the United States is an English-speaking country" (*Guerrero v. Carlson*, 512 P.2d 833, 835 (1973)). The California Supreme Court cited no legal authority for this proposition. (Indeed, it could not have cited any legal authority for this proposition because there is none.) The Court also gave, as one of the bases for its decision, Justice Holmes's declaration that "it is desirable that all citizens of the United States should speak a common tongue." However, the case in which Justice Holmes made such a statement was the *Meyer v. Nebraska* case (see Chapter 1), and his statement, in any event, was part of the dissent. Nonetheless, the California Court's opinion by Justice Mosk found no constitutional basis for notification in Spanish of the termination or reduction of benefits. Justice Tobriner, however, dissented, noting in part:

> In very recent history various cultural subgroups in our society have demanded that they be accorded a legal status not inferior to that which has long been enjoyed by the dominant element. The minorities have attacked the symbols of discrimination, and, to a large extent, and rightly, have succeeded at demolishing them. The law has reflected the social pressure for equal treatment and afforded to the subgroups a new and more meaningful status. One of the sensitive points of the relationship between the minority and the majority elements has been that of language. In many situations the subgroup has been imprisoned within the barrier of inability to communicate in the English language, and because of that handicap has been denied fundamental rights.

Justice Tobriner would have found a constitutional basis for a bilingual notice where welfare workers knew that the recipients did not speak English. He pointed out the 1970 United States Supreme Court case of *Goldberg v. Kelly* which held that recipients of public assistance were entitled under procedural due process to an evidentiary hearing before the state might terminate those payments. Justice Tobriner noted that although the court did not specify the exact form and content of the termination notice in that situation it did declare that the recipient was entitled to timely and adequate notice of a proposed termination. Justice Tobriner would have defined due process to encompass the right of the language minority recipients to a notice in a language they could understand. He would impose a reasonableness test, finding that a state would not need to print notices in all possible languages because it does not know which recipients, if any, speak only those languages, and because there would arguably be so few recipients of some language groups that the expense of translating and printing the notice would be unreasonable.

In another important case, *Carmona v. Sheffield*, the United States Court of Appeals for the Ninth Circuit found that Spanish-speaking citizens were not denied equal protection and due process of the law where the California Department of Human Resources Development conducted its affairs in the English language in the administration of its program of unemployment insurance benefits. The court refused to find a constitutional basis for requiring that interpreters and Spanish language forms be made available to people attempting to obtain unemployment insurance benefits. It concluded that additional burdens which would be imposed on California's finite resources and California's interest in having to deal in only one language with all of its citizens supported the conclusion that the English-only notices and office contact was reasonable.

Another case identifying no constitutional basis for interpretation before administrative agencies is the case of *Frontera v. Sindell*, a decision of the United States Court of Appeals for the Sixth Circuit. In that 1975 decision, Mr. Frontera was a Spanish-speaking carpenter. He had been employed as a carpenter at the Cleveland Hopkins airport under a temporary appointment. He applied for and took the examination for a permanent appointment as a carpenter. The examination was conducted by the city of Cleveland and the commissioner of airports. Mr. Frontera failed to pass the examination and was not certified for appointment. Even though attorneys for both sides stipulated that Frontera had substantial skill as a carpenter, and that the position for which he applied was one of the highest-paid positions in the city of Cleveland, and that he had competently performed his job at the airport under the temporary appointment, he was nonetheless not certified because he failed the test. In his lawsuit, Frontera claimed that he failed because the examination was conducted in English and not in Spanish. He alleged that his Fourteenth Amendment rights to due process and equal protection together with his civil rights under 42 U.S.C. § § 1981, 1983 and 1985 had been violated. In concluding that Mr. Frontera had no right, on a constitutional basis, to a civil service examination in Spanish, the court concluded:

> It cannot be gainsaid that the common, national language of the United States is English. Our laws are printed in English and our legislatures conduct their business in English. Some states even designate English as the official language of the state (citing the Illinois statute). Our national interest in English as the common language is exemplified by 8 U.S.C. § 1423, which requires, in general, English language literacy as a condition to naturalization as a United States citizen.

There are several problems with the court's determination that because English is required for naturalization, English is the national language. First, it ignores the fact that outside the context of naturalization there is no official language. Second, persons seeking naturalization are held to much stricter standards than native-born citizens. For example, people who are mentally insane, retarded, or people who are chronic alcoholics or paupers are all excluded from admission into the United States by the immigration laws (8 U.S.C. § 1182 (1982)). Using the immigration laws to infer a national language would make no more sense than using them to infer this country has a national policy opposed to the mentally retarded. Third, even within the naturalization laws, the standards vary. Those immigrants who are at least fifty years old and who have resided in this country for at least twenty years may take the citizenship examination in the language of their choice (8 U.S.C. § 1423) (1982).

Another case that concludes there is no constitutional right to language assistance in the administrative law context is a 1983 decision of the United States Second Circuit Court of Appeals, entitled *Soberal-Perez v. Heckler.* There the court, citing *Frontera,* determined that there was no constitutional violation where the U.S. Social Security program failed to provide Spanish language forms and instructions to people who had limited English language abilities. While the court concluded that Hispanics do constitute a suspect class (meaning that they should be afforded greater protection under traditional equal protection analysis), the discrimination was not being made, in the court's view, on the basis of race, color, or national origin. The court said the discrimination was on the basis of language, which does not, by itself, according to the court, constitute a suspect class. (For the view that national origin encompasses and protects against language discrimination under Title VII and Title VI of the Civil Rights Act of 1964, and under the United States Constitution, see Chapter 3, the remaining portion of this chapter, and cases cited in Chapter 7 and throughout this book.)

However, the *Soberal-Perez* decision did note that each plaintiff had received a full evidentiary hearing with a translator, and counsel present. Despite the court's conclusion that these plaintiffs had not suffered a violation of any constitutional rights, it left open the question whether due process could, depending upon the circumstances, mandate that particular documents or particular services be afforded in a language other than English.

One important (and apparently inconsistent) exception to the general rule that there is no constitutional right to an interpreter before administrative agencies in this country arises in the immigration context. While in 1903 the U.S. Supreme Court considered an alien's lack of English language ability his or her own misfortune in a deportation proceeding, the current view is that due process requires that an alien be afforded an interpreter in a deportation proceeding.

In another group of cases, it has been held that there is no due process violation where an administrative agency fails to appoint an interpreter, in the absence of a request for one.

Statutory Basis for Interpretation before Administrative Agencies

The cases cited above are often cited quite broadly by opponents of the recognition of language rights for the proposition that administrative agencies are not required to provide language interpretation, and that proceedings resulting in a denial of public assistance, unemployment compensation, and other public assistance need not be concerned with the language barrier of applicants. Such a reading is overbroad. All these cases mean is that administrative agencies are not required, as a constitutional matter, to provide interpretation. It does not mean that administrative agencies are precluded from affording interpreters. In fact, even the majority opinion in _Guerrero_ noted that regulations of the administrative agency in California would have required the provision of an interpreter in an administrative challenge to denial of public assistance. Also in _Guerrero_, the state agency had in fact employed Spanish-speaking personnel to communicate with the plaintiffs and other Spanish-speaking applicants.

Further, there is support for the notion that even though the provision of interpreters may not be constitutionally

required, federal statutes would preclude the exclusion of
language minority applicants from participation in federally funded programs, based solely upon the language barrier. In 1976, for example, the United States District Court
for the Southern District of New York, in a case entitled
Mendoza v. Levine, considered a challenge by language minority applicants against the New York State Department
of Social Services. Plaintiffs were Hispanic persons, who
because of their difficulty with the English language, complained that they received unequal treatment in their applications for public assistance. They alleged that the defendants failed to provide sufficient bilingual personnel,
forms, notices, and applications, so that the plaintiffs in
effect were excluded from participation in a number of
public assistance programs. These programs included Aid
to Families with Dependent Children, Medicaid, and sup-
plemental security income. The first two programs were
partially funded by the federal government through the
Department of Health, Education, and Welfare. The plaintiffs claimed that the policies discriminated against them in
violation of a portion of Title VI of the Civil Rights Act of
1964, 42 U.S.C. § 2000(d). That provision states in part:

> No person in the United States shall, on the ground of race,
> color, or national origin, be excluded from participation in,
> be denied the benefits of, or be subjected to discrimination
> under any program or activity receiving federal financial as-
> sistance.

The plaintiffs also alleged that the discrimination based
upon language violated the Fourteenth Amendment's
equal protection and due process clauses. The court held
that the complaint stated a claim under Title VI and the
Equal Protection and Due Process Clauses which would
survive the defendants' motions to dismiss the cases. The
defendants eventually settled the claims, and seven years
later in 1983 were ordered to pay attorneys' fees to the
plaintiffs' attorneys under the Equal Access to Justice Act.

(Recall that *Lau* and *Serna* were also decided under Title VI. See Chapter 2.)

In addition to furnishing the legal basis for a claim based upon language discrimination, the *Mendoza* case also provides an important study of the effect of the language discrimination that might be successfully used in further litigation. *Guerrero*, for example, found no due process violations, in part because, the court concluded,

> It is also reasonable to assume that in contemporary urban society the non-English-speaking individual has access to a variety of such sources of language assistance. To begin with, he may turn to members of his family, friends or neighbors who are either born in this country or receive some schooling here. If these prove inadequate or unavailable, he may contact representatives of governmental agencies or private organizations . . .

The callousness and damage to families and children in this approach is illustrated by the Mendoza Report. The report was prepared as a result of the complaint by the *Mendoza* plaintiffs. It was a survey of 1,112 cases, or about one percent of all of the Hispanic clients of the New York State Department of Social Services. It was conducted by the United States Department of Health, Education, and Welfare, Office of the Secretary, Office of Civil Rights. It was entitled "Access of Non- or Limited English-Speaking Persons of Hispanic Origin to the New York City Department of Social Services." Completed in 1979, it concluded that the state of New York was in violation of Title VI of the Civil Rights Act of 1964 and the accompanying regulations prohibiting discrimination based on race, color, or national origin. The findings of the report are summarized in an article by Groisser in Volume 16 of the "Columbia Journal of Law and Social Problems." Groisser noted that the statistics cited in the report only pertain to New York, but the problems revealed are shared by all large Hispanic communities in the United States. The report identified three major problem areas.

First, the inadequacy of language translation placed considerable financial burdens on Hispanic families who are receiving public assistance. Families with limited English-speaking heads of households received their welfare checks nearly a week later than did English-speaking clients, resulting in an average loss in 1979 of $75.25 per non–English-speaking family. They also suffered a loss attributable to incidental expenses including transportation for extra trips to welfare offices, extra child care costs, lost wages, payments for interpreters, translation, notarization of documents and other expenses.

Second, the report concluded that the practice among non–English-speaking clients of using children as interpreters could potentially inflict considerable psychological and emotional damage on Hispanic families. Quite apart from the loss of school days, the report emphasized that psychological research could be expected to show that damage would be inflicted on children when they are prematurely burdened with the vital responsibility of being the determining factor in insuring the economic survival of the family. They would be exposed to harm and stress when they served as the conduit through which their parents are cross-examined concerning intimate matters. Parents would undoubtedly feel guilt and anxiety over these effects. Further, even where a child was not used, parents would feel an invasion of privacy in requiring a friend to sit in during a session with a welfare worker.

Third, the report found that the majority of non–English-speaking clients were given no information, in any language, concerning additional welfare services such as obtaining and enforcing a fair hearing, or securing free community legal, housekeeping, education, or day care assistance.

The report concluded that there had in fact been a violation of the statute and regulations, concluding that because of language barriers, nearly a third of qualified applicants were forced to both absorb costs unknown to the remainder of the population and to wait longer periods of time to receive their benefits. This type of study and litigation would undoubtedly be of assistance to potential plaintiffs in other administrative agency actions.

Other cases as well indicate that courts will find statutory, or perhaps eventually a constitutional right to bilingual assistance in administrative proceedings. In *Pabon v. Levine*, for example, the U.S. District Court for the Southern District of New York considered the claim of a plaintiff who brought a class action suit against the New York State Department of Labor, alleging that the department's practice of printing all materials related to unemployment benefits in English violated Title VI. The court held the claim sufficient to withstand a motion for summary judgment, although the court denied class certification and did not ultimately reach the claim of discrimination. (In 1978, as was noted in Chapter 2, the U.S. Supreme Court arguably decided that a claim under Title VI was coextensive with the claim of a violation of the Equal Protection Clause of the Fourteenth Amendment, although this point of law is still unresolved.)

Where a language disability prevents an applicant before an administrative body from taking advantage of the right to counsel, courts have been even more sympathetic in finding a violation of the plaintiff's rights resulting from a lack of bilingual assistance. For example, in *Rosa v. Weinberger*, a Spanish-speaking claimant was found not to have waived her right to counsel at a Social Security disability hearing where the notice of the hearing had been in English and the claimant was permitted to labor under the misconception that 25 percent of her back benefits would be withheld as compensation if she were to obtain an attorney. Similarly, in *Cortez v. Weinberger*, a disability claimant was found to be entitled to a rehearing on the grounds that a lack of an attorney and an interpreter was unfair because it appeared that a fully comprehending claimant could have made a stronger presentation of his case.

Language minority individuals and their advocates may have to be somewhat resourceful in identifying their exclusion from programs and gathering authority for the proposition that such exclusion is unlawful or unethical. By definition, the person who does not speak English is going to be hindered in an attempt to learn, through English language sources, of even the existence of some programs. One such instance that comes to mind, based upon the author's experience, is the research conducted upon human subjects by medical schools and drug companies. Some of these studies involve great risks with little benefit to individual subjects. Others, however, may provide cash payments, free medication and medical treatment, and other benefits with relatively minor risks. Federal regulations provide that any clinical investigation that must meet the requirements for "prior submission to the Food and Drug Administration" shall not be initiated unless that investigation has been reviewed and approved by, and remains subject to, continuing review by an institutional review board (21 C.F.R. 56.103 (1988)). The Belmont Report, a federally funded study published in the Federal Register, requires in part that institutional review boards distribute the benefits of institutional research in a just fashion, taking into account racial, sexual, and cultural biases in society. This author concludes that Title VI, and its accompanying regulations, requires that any medical facility receiving federal funding that engages in medical research with benefit to participating subjects must not arbitrarily deny benefits of the research to potential language minority participants. Otherwise, it is foreseeable that important benefits, such as the extension of life of a terminally ill patient, might be denied to a person who does not happen to speak English or to a child whose parents happen not to speak English.

In these, and similar cases, the lack of clear constitutional authority requiring the appointment of interpreters before administrative agencies has not stopped plaintiffs and their counsel from bringing claims inside and outside of court. In 1974, for example, even after the *Guerrero* decision, Spanish-speaking litigants in northern California brought a

lawsuit alleging they were not afforded public social service benefits on an equal basis with non-Spanish speakers
because of the lack of adequate bilingual staff. The lawsuit
was settled, with the government agency agreeing to provide adequate bilingual staff and implementing procedures
to identify people whose language barriers might preclude
them from receiving assistance. Two years later, the state of
Illinois agreed, in settlement of a similar case, to furnish
timely notice and adequate explanations in Spanish as well
as providing hearings to Spanish-speaking persons who
were filing unemployment insurance claims under either
federal or state unemployment insurance acts.

Beyond the pressing of judicial claims for relief, of
course, non-English speakers and their advocates might
also consider appealing to the federal funding source of
state social service programs in an effort to enforce compliance with applicable statutes and regulations which preclude the absolute exclusion of language minority participants. The *Mendoza* report is the result of such an appeal.
Under the current Title VI regulations, persons who believe they have been subjected to unlawful national origin
discrimination may file a written complaint with the Department of Health and Human Services within 180 days
from the date of the discrimination (the deadline can be
extended). There can be no retaliation against such com-
plainants. If there appears to be a failure or threatened
failure to comply with the prohibition against national
origin discrimination, and if it cannot be corrected by informal means, compliance may be effected by the suspension
or termination of federal financial assistance. The matter
may be referred to the Justice Department for further legal
action. The potential cutoff of federal funding can be a
powerful tool in resisting language discrimination before
administrative agencies.

Unfortunately, however, Title VI only applies to situations where federal funding is given to a nonfederal entity
which, in turn, provides financial assistance to an ultimate
beneficiary. As a result, programs involving direct pay-

ments from the federal government are not covered. As an ironic result, while the U.S. Department of Health and Human Services will investigate and sanction nonfederal agencies that engage in language discrimination (*Mendoza*), that agency itself has successfully resisted the efforts of potential recipients of Social Security who sought not to be excluded by a language barrier (*Soberal-Perez*).

As a concluding note, some federal agencies explicitly recognize language protections, as will be briefly discussed in Chapter 7.

Bibliography

Articles

1. Groisser, *A Right to Translation Assistance in Administrative Proceedings*, 16 Colum. J.L. & Soc. Probs. 469 (1981).
2. Piatt, *Toward Domestic Recognition of a Human Right to Language*, 23 Hous. L. Rev. 885 (1986).
3. Comment, *Citado A Comparecer: Language Barriers and Due Process—Is Mailed Notice in English Constitutionally Sufficient*, 61 Calif. L. Rev. 1395 (1973).
4. Note, *El Derecho de Aviso: Due Process and Bilingual Notice*, 83 Yale L.J. 385 (1973).

Federal Constitutional Provision, Statute, Regulation

U.S. Const. amend. XIV.
Title III, Civil Rights Act of 1964, 42 U.S.C. 2000d (1981).
21 C.F.R. 56.103 (1988).
45 C.F.R. 80 (1988).

Selected Federal Judicial Decisions

1. *Asociation Mixta Progresista v. HEW*, Pov. L. Rep. (CCH) ¶ 20,335 (N.D. Cal. 1974).

2. *Carmona v. Sheffield*, 475 F.2d 738 (9th Cir. 1973).
3. *Cortez v. Weinberger*, Pov. L. Rep. (CCH) ¶ 22,347 (E.D. Pa. 1975).
4. *Frontera v. Sindell*, 522 F.2d 1215 (6th Cir. 1975).
5. *Mendoza v. Lavine*, 412 F. Supp. 1105 (S.D.N.Y. 1976), 91 F.R.D. 91 (1981), 560 F. Supp. 284 (1983).
6. *Pabon v. Levine*, 70 F.R.D. 674 (S.D.N.Y. 1976).
7. *Rosa v. Weinberger*, 381 F. Supp. 377 (E.D.N.Y. 1974).
8. *Soto v. Johnson*, Pov. L. Rep. (CCH) ¶ 23,345 (N.D. Ill. 1976).
9. *Tejeda-Mata v. I.N.S.*, 626 F.2d 721 (1980) (Right to interpreter in deportation).
10. *Yamataya v. Fisher*, 189 U.S. 86 (1903) (lack of English understanding alien's own misfortune).

Selected State Judicial Decisions

County Trust Co. v. Mora, 87 Misc. 2d 11, 383 N.Y.S.2d 468 (1975).
Guerrero v. Carlson, 9 Cal. 3d 808, 512 P.2d 833, 109 Cal. Rptr. 201 (1973).
Ramsey v. Ross, 405 N.Y.S.2d 808 (1978).

Other Sources

U.S. Dept. of H.E.W., Office of the Sec'y, Office of Civil Rights, Access of Non- or Limited-English-Speaking Persons of Hispanic Origin to the N.Y.C. Dep't of Social Services (1979) ("Mendoza Report"), cited in Groisser, supra.

Chapter 6

Broadcasting

In our examination of language rights issues thus far, we have examined situations where a lack of language assistance can have immediate and potentially devastating impact upon people in this country who do not speak English. One might wonder at the inclusion of a discussion of foreign language broadcasting in connection with an examination of the human right to language. After all, isn't broadcasting basically only entertainment? The answer is that, as we will discover in this chapter, broadcasting represents much more than entertainment. This is particularly true regarding television, especially when the audience consists of children, and more particularly, when the audience consists of minority children.

Early Views of the Desirability of Foreign-Language Broadcasting

Unlike printed media, the nature of broadcasting requires that some regulatory decisions be made regarding the utilization of broadcast power and frequencies. Otherwise, a clutter of signals would result. Recognizing this reality, Congress passed the Radio Act of 1927. The act established the Federal Radio Commission (FRC) and authorized it to assign bands of frequency or wavelengths to various classes of stations and to individual stations. The FRC was also empowered to determine the broadcast power each station would be authorized to use, and the time of day or night during which it would operate. All of these decisions were to be made using the test of the requirements of public convenience, interest, or necessity.

In an early case, the FRC and the courts were called upon to determine the appropriateness of foreign language broadcasting in this country. The issue arose in the context of competing applications for a broadcast frequency in the Gary, Indiana, area in the early 1930s. In deciding the case, the FRC ruled in favor of a broadcaster supplying foreign language broadcasting. The decision was upheld in 1933 by the United States Supreme Court (*FRC v. Nelson Bros.*). The Court noted that Gary, Indiana, is located in a region which had a population at that time of about 800,000. Sixty percent of those people were foreign-born, representing over fifty nationalities. The radio station in question, WJKS, was providing programs which the FRC and court concluded were well-designed to meet the needs of the foreign population. These programs included broadcasts for Hungarian, Italian, Mexican, Spanish, German, Russian, Polish, Croatian, Lithuanian, Scotch and Irish people, and were musical, educational and instructive in their nature, and "stressed loyalty to the community and the Nation" (289 U.S. 266, 271 (1933)). Programs were arranged and supervised "to stimulate community and racial origin pride and rivalry and to instruct in citizenship and American ideals and responsibilities" (Id). "Special safety prevention talks" (Id) were given for workingmen, explaining the application of new safeguards of various types of machinery used in the steel mills. The children's hour utilized selections from various schools. There were "good citizenship talks" (Id) weekly by civic leaders. The facilities of the station were made available to the local police department and to all fraternal, charitable, and religious organizations in the region, without charge. Sunday programs consisted mainly of church service broadcasts including all churches and denominations desiring to participate. The FRC, with judicial approach, concluded that this programming constituted excellent public service.

In 1934, Congress enacted a new Communications Act. The act created the successor to the FRC, the Federal Communications Commission (FCC). The FCC was directed to grant broadcast licenses to applicants "if public convenience, interest, or necessity will be served thereby." (47 U.S.C. § 307(a) (1976)). In 1935 the FCC expressed disapproval of foreign language broadcasts ("Jewish, Italian and Polish") which were primarily advertising programs stressing the sale of merchandise in the Brooklyn area (*U.S. Broadcasting Corp.*, 2 F.C.C. 208, 223 (1935)).

Neither the 1927 nor 1934 acts made any mention of foreign language broadcasting. Nor did those acts delineate what exactly would constitute broadcasting in the public interest, although the U.S. Supreme Court in 1943 held that *public interest* meant the interest of the listening public in the "larger and more effective use of radio."

Contemporary View: Does the FCC Require Foreign-Language Broadcasting?

No statute or regulation now exists requiring broadcasters specifically to present any portion of programming in a foreign language. The FCC and the courts, however, have generally recognized the desirability of such programming and occasionally speak in terms of an obligation on the part of broadcasters to provide it, although there is much inconsistency.

In the 1950s and 1960s, the FCC discussed foreign language broadcasting in the context of cases wherein one applicant for a broadcast license sought preference over another on the basis that it had more of a commitment to serve the foreign language audience. In 1956 the FCC, with judicial approval, granted an application to an applicant who wished to operate a television station. The applicant already operated a radio station, and the fact that it was broadcasting in Spanish in the Tampa, Florida, area was given favorable consideration in the decision to award a television license to the same applicant. Two years later, however, the FCC vacillated. An applicant in another case sought to present 5.8 percent of its total programming in foreign languages. The FCC this time found a detriment existed to those who would not be able to comprehend the programming and found that detriment would outweigh the benefit to those who needed and wanted it. Therefore the FCC found no basis for giving the applicant preference over another broadcaster who proposed less foreign language programming. In 1966, however, an applicant proposed to present an all-Spanish radio format in Lubbock, Texas. That applicant was given preference by the FCC over another which only sought to broadcast part-time in Spanish. The FCC rejected its hearing examiners' determination that all-Spanish programming would be inconsistent with state and national policy. It then applied a two-pronged analysis: (1) do a substantial number of persons residing within the proposed service area lack the ability to comprehend English, or is their working knowledge of English so poor that for purposes of public service announcements they can be reached effectively only by an all-Spanish language station? (2) to what extent would the proposed programming meet such need? The FCC relied upon testimony of a growing Latin American population in the Lubbock, Texas area, 60 to 80 percent of which could not properly understand English, in finding a need for full-time Spanish programming, and awarded the license to the full-time Spanish station.

In 1967, a public pronouncement by the FCC warned broadcasters to maintain adequate control over foreign language programs. A clarifying memorandum in 1973 acknowledged the desirability of foreign language programming, noting that "we [FCC] have never held or implied that foreign language programming should be denied when a demonstrable need for it exists." (39 F.C.C. 2d 1037 (1973)). However, the memo did not address the issue of when or how broadcasters would be required to meet the demonstrated need. A second clarification in 1983 eliminated the control requirements, acknowledged the need for more foreign language programming, and encouraged time sharing to provide such programming, but still failed to discuss any obligation on the part of broadcasters to provide it.

The language issue has also arisen in license renewal challenges. Deficiencies in service to the Mexican-American community was a factor in a 1981 decision to limit the license renewal of the New Mexico Broadcasting Company to one year. Although petitioners raised the failure to provide broadcasting in the Spanish language, there was no specific finding by the FCC on this issue.

The language in broadcasting issue has arisen in a couple of other contexts as well. The FCC has considered several ironic cases where one Spanish language broadcaster seeks to limit access to the airwaves by a potential competitor who also seeks to broadcast in Spanish. In another case, arising in Tucson in 1971, the federal court, reviewing the actions of the FCC, explicitly acknowledged that there could be a failure to serve a language minority group that cannot understand the English language broadcasting in a geographic area. The FCC reexamined the case, concluding that if a substantial segment of the community thinks and speaks in the Spanish language only, and cannot understand the English language, broadcast stations in the area must be responsive.

Should the FCC Require Foreign Language Broadcasting?

As in other contexts, there are inconsistent case holdings and results in the FCC's struggle with the issue of foreign language broadcasting. Further exploration of these inconsistent cases and regulations can be found in this author's 1984 article entitled "Linguistic Diversity on the Airwaves: Spanish Language Broadcasting and the FCC," which is cited in the bibliography. These inconsistencies may well be the result of the general societal ambiguity regarding the acceptance of other languages discussed throughout this book.

Despite the regulatory ambivalence, the marketplace is producing what can only be described as an explosion in the Spanish language media. Univision, a Spanish language television network, now counts over 465 affiliated stations and cable systems in this country. A new Spanish language network, Telemundo, has begun broadcasting in the United States. These cable outlets are joined by the increasing availability of Spanish language home videos in providing Spanish language television viewing opportunities in this country. In terms of pure entertainment, it would appear that at least the Spanish language audience is being served, and perhaps the FCC need not impose any foreign language requirement upon traditional broadcast facilities.

On the other hand, traditional broadcast facilities of television and radio licensed by the FCC continue to supply the bulk of local news coverage, information about local community events, and other programming aimed at local audiences. The presence of English language cable stations serving particularized needs has not resulted in a decision by the FCC to ignore its regulatory functions in requiring local broadcasters to provide programming in English to serve the local public interest. Similarly, the presence of cable Spanish language programming should not cause the FCC to abandon efforts to determine when local stations should provide foreign language broadcasting in the local public interest. More specifically, after reviewing the cases, regulations, and various studies, it is this author's conclusion that there are at least four reasons why local foreign language broadcasting should be made available, by FCC requirement if necessary.

1. *Interests of monolingual foreign language speakers*

Broadcast licensees must serve the public interest. While broadcasters have wide discretion in selecting community needs to be addressed by their programming, both the FCC and the courts have held that a broadcaster must take into consideration the problems of minorities in the communities in which he or she is licensed to serve, or suffer the loss or restriction of the broadcast license. Where the minority community speaks only Spanish (or any other language), failure of broadcasters to provide foreign language broadcasting constitutes a complete failure to serve that group. (This is the *Tucson* approach.)

2. *Interests of bilingual members of the broadcast audience*

Even if they also understand English, Hispanic-Americans or other language minority groups have an important interest in receiving foreign language broadcasting to maintain contact with and improve upon their language abilities. Failure of broadcasters to make Spanish broadcasting available to bilingual Hispanics, for example, creates an insensitive and hostile broadcast climate which has a strong potential negative impact, particularly upon Hispanic children.

This conclusion regarding the negative impact upon Hispanics, especially children, is supported by several studies. A 1979 report of the United States Commission on Civil Rights concluded, for example, that all groups of children are impressionable. Many use television to inform themselves about real life. However, low income minority children show a somewhat greater tendency to accept television as real than do middle income, majority children. Also, testimony presented in a 1981 case involving a broadcast license in New Mexico indicated that as a result of Hispanic children seeing few Hispanic role models on television, and as a result of the exclusion of their language and culture from television programming, these children often feel that there is something inferior about their language and culture, and consequently, about themselves and their families.

This testimony by Dr. Rupert A. Trujillo, Dean of Continuing Education and Community Services at the University of New Mexico, was further supported by the testimony of Professor Antonio Mondragon of the Department of Psychology at the University of New Mexico. According to Professor Mondragon, the culture and values of the Mexican-American population have been misinterpreted by the Anglo culture and a majority of the American people. This lack of understanding, on the part of society as a whole, has had a negative impact on the Mexican-American self-image. Professor Mondragon concluded this problem could be alleviated if the media would portray positive role models. He concluded the media should also ensure the proper pronunciation of Hispanic names, and refrain from negative editorializing of news stories of interest to Mexican-Americans. As a result of the testimony of Dr. Trujillo, Professor Mondragon, and others, a broadcast license renewal was limited to only one year due to the failure of the broadcaster to meet the needs of the Hispanic community in New Mexico.

These experts and others (see, for example, the New Mexico Broadcasting case, cited in the bibliography), have concluded that cultural and linguistic insensitivity on the part of the media creates a not necessarily deliberate, but nonetheless hostile, environment. The hostile environment can result in problems of self-image, which in turn, affects the educational dropout rate of Mexican-American children.

3.   *Interests of monolingual English speakers*

Non–foreign-language-speaking individuals, Hispanics and non-Hispanics alike, may have an interest in acquiring language skills and greater cultural diversity by having access to foreign language broadcasting. The FCC has recognized that minority programming benefits the nonminority community as well: Adequate representation of minority community as well: "Adequate representation of minority needs and interests of the minority community, but also enriches and educates the non-minority audience." (See

Statement of Policy on Minority Ownership of Broadcast Facilities, cited in the bibliography.) The notion that monolingual English speakers in this country benefit from the presence of other cultures is explored in Chapter 9 of this book.

4. *A First Amendment right?*

Finally, foreign-language-speaking audiences may have a First Amendment right to foreign language broadcasting. In upholding the FCC's former Fairness Doctrine (requiring broadcasters to give equal time to individuals personally attacked in broadcasts and to political opponents of station-endorsed candidates), the U.S. Supreme Court found a First Amendment free speech right in the listening public. It found that because of the scarcity of broadcast frequencies, the government is permitted to put restraints on licenses. But it found that the people as a whole:

> retain their interest in free speech by radio and their collective right to have the medium function consistently with the ends and purposes of the First Amendment. It is the right of the viewers and listeners, not the right of the broadcasters, which is paramount. It is the right of the public to receive suitable access to social, political, esthetic, moral, and other ideas and experiences which is crucial here. (*Red Lion* case, cited in bibliography).

Obviously, when broadcasting is only in English, the exclusively foreign-language-speaking listener has no suitable access to the ideas, experiences, views, and voices which the Court finds to be his or her right. We recognize that other rights cannot be effectively exercised unless some accommodation is made for language differences: bilingual education (Chapter 2), the provision of interpreters for litigants and witnesses (Chapter 4), and the requirement that Miranda warnings be given in an understandable language (Chapter 7) are examples. There is no apparent reason why the First Amendment right recognized in the *Red Lion* case would be any less important.

People who do understand English and do therefore have access to English language broadcasting may still have a First Amendment right to a diversified programming schedule that would include foreign language broadcasting. The Statement of Policy on Minority Ownership of Broadcasting Facilities noted above also indicates that diversified programming is a key objective not only in the Communications Act of 1934, but also of the First Amendment.

We should note, however, before leaving this point, that in August 1987, the FCC, under Chairman Dennis Patrick, abolished the Fairness Doctrine. President Reagan subsequently vetoed a congressionally approved law which would have reinstated it. President Bush is on record as stating he would veto any subsequent Fairness Doctrine law passed by Congress. The *Red Lion* case, although never overturned, has thus been limited by repeal of the Fairness Doctrine, and criticized by subsequent judicial and scholarly discussions. The apparently broad First Amendment guarantee it affords the listening public may now be open to debate.

Remedies for Persons Adversely Affected by a Lack of Foreign Language Programming

The ambivalence and uncertainty in the FCC and the courts certainly does not leave persons adversely affected by a lack of foreign language programming without a remedy. Such persons and groups should seriously consider the suggestions of the United States District Court for the District of Columbia in the *Tucson* case. The court implied that among the remedies for the failure of broadcast stations to provide foreign language broadcasting would be for persons desiring such service to: (1) request such service from existing broadcast stations; (2) attempt to bring the need for such programming to the attention of stations and the Federal Communications Commission through challenges to license renewals; or (3) file competing applications for the broadcast license. The New Mexico Broadcasting case should also offer encouragement and a guideline for an effective approach to this problem.

People and groups interested in these issues should also be aware of constructive alternatives that can produce a win-win result for broadcasters, the general public, and the language minority audience as well. Among these is the recognition that in some market areas, including Albuquerque and Dallas, broadcasters are succeeding in fulfilling their obligations to the Spanish language community (and presumably increasing their audiences and revenues as well) by news simulcasts with a local Spanish language radio station. Spanish-speaking television viewers who wish to understand the English language local television news can turn down the volume on the T.V. set, and tune to a radio station which, by arrangement with the T.V. station, provides a simultaneous translation of the broadcast.

Local cable companies might also be persuaded to carry foreign language networks if approached in a constructive fashion. In attempting to persuade the local cable television company in Topeka, Kansas, to include a Spanish language network, this author succeeded in the endeavor in 1984 by gathering signatures from a large number of potential new subscribers who were able to convince the company that increased profits would flow from the provision of service to this group.

Bibliography

Articles

1. Bowie and Whitehead, *The Federal Communication Commission's Equal Employment Opportunity Regulation—An Agency in Search of a Standard*, 5 Black L.J. 313 (1977).

2. Canby, *Programming in Response to the Community, the Broadcast Consumer and the First Amendment*, 55 Tex. L. Rev. 67 (1976).
3. McNeil, *The Right to Cultural Pluralism in Broadcasting*, 6 Black L.J. 232 (1978–79).
4. Piatt, *Linguistic Diversity on the Airwaves: Spanish Language Broadcasting and the FCC*, 1 La Raza L.J. 101 (1984).
5. Note, *Use of Petitions by Minority Groups to Deny Broadcast License Renewals*, 1978 Duke L.J. 271.

Federal Constitutional Provisions, Statutes, Regulations

U.S. Const. amend. I.
Communications Act of 1934, 47 U.S.C. § 151 (1962).
47 C.F.R. § 73 (1987).
Radio Act of 1927, 44 Stat. 1166, 45 Stat. 373.

Selected Federal Judicial and FCC Decisions

1. *Alabama Educational Television Commission*, 50 F.C.C. 2d 461 (1975) (failure to serve needs of Black community constitutes failure of license responsibility irrespective of intent to discriminate).
2. *Federal Radio Commission v. Nelson Bros. Bond & Morgtgage Co.*, 289 U.S. 266 (1933).
3. *In re Great Lakes Television, Inc.*, 25 F.C.C. 470 (1958).
4. *In Re La Fiesta Broadcasting Co.*, 6 F.C.C. 2d 65 (1966).
5. *National Broadcasting Co. v. United States*, 319 U.S. 190 (1943) (FCC to ensure broadcast in the public interest; public interest defined).
6. *New Mexico Broadcasting Co.*, 87 F.C.C. 2d 213 (1981).
7. *Red Lion Broadcasting Co., v. F.C.C.*, 395 U.S. 367 (1969).
8. *Tampa Times Co. v. F.C.C.*, 19 F.C.C. 257 (1954), *aff'd*, 230 F.2d 224 (D.C. Cir. 1956).
9. *Tucson Radio, Inc. v. F.C.C.*, 24 F.C.C. 2d at 829, 452 F.2d 1380 (D.C. Cir. 1971).
10. *United States Broadcasting Corp.*, 2 F.C.C. 208 (1935).

Other Authorities

Foreign Language Programs: Broadcasters Cautioned to Exercise Adequate Control, 32 Fed. Reg. 64 (1967).

Licensee Responsibility to Exercise Adequate Control Over Foreign Language Programs, 39 F.C.C. 2d 1037 (1973).

Elimination of Unnecessary Broadcast Regulations and Subscription Agreements Between Radio Broadcast Stations and Music Format Service Companies, 48 Fed. Reg. 49, 852 (1983).

Statement of Policy on Minority Ownership of Broadcast Facilities, 8 F.C.C. 2d 979 (1978).

U.S. Commission on Civil Rights, Window Dressing on the Set: An Update (1979).

Chapter 7

Scattered Seeds of Language Rights

Our legal system recognizes language rights in a number of contexts, in addition to those which we have already examined. In this chapter, we will consider various other areas. Grouping them into one chapter does not mean they are insignificant. Rather, it is a concession to the reality that the recognition of language rights in this country is inconsistent. An attempt, in the subsequent chapters of this book, to analyze these inconsistencies and consider alternatives nonetheless requires us to understand the existence of, and the basis for, the many areas where the seeds of recognition of a human right to language have germinated. Grouping a number of other language rights areas into this chapter is also a concession to space and time limitations and the author's interest in reserving enough of the reader's interest to engage in an analysis and overview in subsequent chapters.

Yu Cong Eng

An important case supporting the principle that there is a constitutional right to use a language other than the official language of a state can be found in a 1926 decision of the United States Supreme Court. This decision, though never reversed, has gone virtually unnoticed by both proponents and opponents of "official English" provisions.

In February 1921 the Philippine legislature approved an act making it unlawful for any person in the Philippine Islands to keep account books in any language other than English, Spanish, or a local dialect. It imposed criminal sanctions upon violators. Those convicted could be punished by a fine of not more than ten thousand *pesos* or by imprisonment for not more than two years, or both. The act took effect on January 1, 1923.

Yu Cong Eng was a Chinese merchant engaged in a wholesale lumber business in Manila. He neither read, wrote, nor understood English, Spanish, or any local Philippine dialect. As a result, he kept his books in the Chinese characters he understood. He was charged with a violation of the Philippine Act and appealed his conviction to the United States Supreme Court. (The political relationship between the Philippine Islands and the United States at that time provided for such a review.) In the Supreme Court, Mr. Eng, through his attorneys, argued that because of his ignorance of English, Spanish, and other languages and dialects in use in the Philippines, he could not keep his books in any language other than Chinese. He argued that even if he should employ a bookkeeper capable of keeping his books in the English language, he would have no means of personally revising or ascertaining the contents or correctness of the books and would be completely at the mercy of such employees who, if dishonest, might cheat and defraud him. (Remember Professor Player's suggestion noted in Chapter 3 that an employer who does not speak English should be required to hire an interpreter rather than deny employment opportunities to employees who speak only English?) He alleged that the enforcement of the law would drive him and many other Chinese merchants in the Philippines out of doing business in the islands. He argued that the application of the law would violate his constitutionally protected rights to due process and equal protection of the laws.

The government of the Philippines answered that the law was a valid and necessary exercise of a proper legislative power. It argued that due to the inability of the officials of the Philippines' Internal Revenue Service to properly check upon the correctness of the books of account kept by Chinese merchants in their own language, the public treasury was losing very large sums of money each year. The Supreme Court was thus faced with the classic confrontation between the individual right to use a native language of choice, and the interest of an English- (or Spanish) speaking majority to enforce the use of an official tongue.

The U.S. Supreme Court, citing *Meyer v. Nebraska* (see Chapter 2), found the Philippine law to be a violation of the due process and equal protection rights of Yu Cong Eng. In analyzing the issue, the Court noted that Chinese merchants had been in the Philippines even before the arrival of the Spaniards and later the English (just as Hispanics in this country can trace the arrival of their Spanish-speaking forebears to a date prior to the arrival of English-speaking colonists). The Court concluded that in view of the history of the islands and the conditions prevailing there, the law was invalid because it deprives Chinese persons situated as they are, with their extensive and important business long-established, of their liberty and property without due process of law, and denies them the equal protection of the laws. Accordingly, the U.S. Supreme Court upheld the Philippine Supreme Court's decision that the statute was invalid.

Application of the Civil Rights Acts to Private Language Discrimination Outside the Workplace

In 1972, two Mexican-Americans went to a tavern in Forest Grove, Oregon, where a bartender served them beer. While drinking, the three men began conversing in Spanish, their native tongue. Anglo customers who were also sitting at the bar became irritated and complained to the bartender. The bartender advised the Mexican-Americans that if they persisted in speaking Spanish they would have to go to a booth or leave the premises, in accordance with a rule of the bar which stated: "Do not allow a foreign language to be used at the bar if it interferes with the regular trade. If there should be a chance of a problem, ask the 'problem' people to move to a table and turn the juke box up (use house money)" (*Hernandez v. Erlenbusch*, cited in the bibliography, at p. 752). The Mexican-Americans took issue with the order and an argument ensued. The bartender poured out the remaining beer and refused to refund any money. The police were called and the Mexican-Americans left peaceably.

Two days later, the scene was reenacted with different plaintiffs. The bartender pulled the beers of three Mexican-Americans. The Mexican-Americans were then followed out of the tavern and assaulted by three Anglo customers. The bartender later testified that she agreed with, and willingly enforced the rule. The Anglo patrons concurred, saying they knew of the rule and wholeheartedly endorsed it. The bar owner testified he had adopted the policy simply to avoid trouble and to preserve his liquor license.

The Mexican-Americans were obviously not satisfied with the existence and application of the rule, and brought suit under the Reconstruction Era Civil Rights Acts. The court found in favor of the Mexican-American plaintiffs. It began its opinion as follows:

> The events in August 1972 which produced this case took place in a nondescript little tavern in Forest Grove. They involve nothing more—nor less—lofty than the right of some American citizens to enjoy a bottle of beer at the tavern bar and to speak in Spanish while doing so. The fact that the case was brought is indicative that our society has made significant progress in casting off the more overt forms of racial discrimination. The actions in the tavern—and immediately

outside—are, however, a sad reminder that significant racially discriminatory attitudes still remain.

The court concluded that the rule as intended and applied deprives Spanish-speaking persons of the rights to buy, drink, and enjoy what the tavern has to offer on an equal footing with English-speaking customers. It found that the plaintiffs' rights under 42 U.S.C. § 1981, ("to make and enforce contracts and to the full and equal benefit of all laws, as is enjoyed by white citizens") had been violated. It also found a violation of their § 1982 guarantee that "all citizens of the United States shall have the same right to purchase personal property." The property involved in this case was a bottle of beer. The deprivation of this property right, it concluded, was the same deprivation that courts had identified as being impermissible where the property involved was a house, or even a ticket to a recreational event. It identified the principle as being the same as that involved in civil rights lunch counter sit-ins and bus cases of the 1960s. The court went on:

> Just as the Constitution forbids banishing blacks to the back of the bus so as not to arouse the racial animosity of the preferred white passengers, it also forbids ordering Spanish-speaking patrons to the 'back booth or out' to avoid antagonizing English-speaking beer drinkers.
>
> The lame justification that a discriminatory policy helps preserve the peace is as unacceptable in barrooms as it was in buses. Catering to prejudice out of fear of provoking greater prejudice only perpetuates racism. Courts faithful to the Fourteenth Amendment will not permit, either by camouflage or cavalier treatment, equal protection so to be profaned.

The court concluded that the plaintiffs would each recover one hundred dollars for the humiliation and distress resulting from the discriminatory language policy. The plaintiff who was actually physically attacked was awarded a total of approximately five hundred dollars in damages.

Miranda Warnings in an Understandable Language

In 1965 the United States Supreme Court ruled in *Miranda v. Arizona* that under the Fifth Amendment to the United States Constitution, because an individual is not compelled to incriminate himself or herself, a person in police custody must, prior to interrogation, be clearly informed of certain rights. Those rights include the fact that the suspect has the right to remain silent, and that anything he or she says can and will be used against him or her in court. He or she must also be informed that there is a right to consult with an attorney and to have the lawyer present during interrogation. If the suspect is indigent, a lawyer will be appointed to represent him or her.

The issue has arisen as to the validity of these warnings when a person who does not speak English hears the warnings in the English language. In such cases, the courts have concluded that there can be no effective waiver of the privilege against self-incrimination unless the accused is given the warnings in a language he or she understands.

Voting Rights Act of 1965

One harsh legal reality in the United States is that for almost two centuries, various state governments built a host of obstacles aimed at denying minority citizens of this country the right to vote. Minority persons, for example, were required to pay poll taxes, pass literacy tests, give oral interpretations of the Constitution, and pass moral and character tests in many instances before being allowed to vote. Some states even required a white man to vouch for the character and the morality of a potential minority voter before that person would even be allowed to register. Minority voters, even if registered, were required to sit for several hours answering questions of interpretations of constitutional law while white voters entered the poll-

ing place without molestation. Such discriminatory tech-
niques, together with open intimidation and violence, operated to exclude minorities from participation in voting.
(See the Report of the House Judiciary Subcommittee No.
5, Hearings on H.R. 6400, 89th Congress, 1st Session,
1965.) Civil rights legislation in 1957, 1960, and 1964 sought
to expand the right to vote. As a practical matter, however,
they had little impact.

In 1965, however, at the height of civil rights consciousness, protest, and violence, Congress enacted what has
been described as possibly the most radical piece of civil
rights legislation since Reconstruction. The Voting Rights
Act sought to prevent minority voting exclusion. It sought
to enforce the Fifteenth Amendment's prohibition against
the denial of the right to vote by states on the basis of race,
color, or previous condition of servitude. As President
Johnson noted, it sought "to eliminate every remaining
obstacle to the right and opportunity to vote." The act has
been amended several times since 1965 and remains a
rather complex piece of legislation.

The act explicitly recognizes the difficulties facing language minority citizens who seek to exercise their right to
vote:

> The Congress finds that voting discrimination against cit-
> izens of language minorities is pervasive and national in
> scope. Such minority citizens are from environments in
> which the dominant language is other than English. In addi-
> tion, they have been denied equal educational opportunity
> by state and local governments, resulting in severe dis-
> abilities and continuing illiteracy in the English language.
> The Congress further finds that, where state and local offi-
> cials conduct elections only in English, language minority
> citizens are excluded from participating in the electoral pro-
> cess. In many areas of the country, this exclusion is aggra-
> vated by acts of physical, economic, and political
> intimidation. Congress declares that, in order to enforce the
> guarantees of the Fourteenth and Fifteenth Amendments to
> the United States Constitution, it is necessary to eliminate

such discrimination by prohibiting English-only elections, and by prescribing other remedial devices.

The act goes on to prohibit any practice or procedure which is imposed to deny the right of any citizen of the United States to vote because he or she is a member of a language minority group. Again, while the act is complicated, there are two major provisions which provide a requirement for bilingual voting materials.

First, under what is referred to as Section 4(f) (4), a state or political subdivision subject to the act must provide any registration or voting notices, forms, instruction, assistance, or other materials or information relating to the electoral process, including ballots, in the language of the applicable language minority group as well as in the English language. (Where the language of the applicable minority group is oral or unwritten or historically unwritten, the state or political subdivision is only required to furnish oral instructions, assistance, or other information.) This provision applies to any state or political subdivision in which: (1) over five percent of the voting age citizens were, on November 1, 1972, members of a single language minority group; (2) registration and election materials were provided only in English on November 1, 1972; and (3) fewer than fifty percent of the voting age citizens were registered to vote or voted in the 1972 presidential election. Again, while the act and regulations are complicated, states may obtain a judicial determination that they are not covered under these requirements if during the ten years prior to filing of the action and during the pendency of the action, they can show, in effect, that there has been no application of measures with the effect or intent of abridging the right to vote.

Another section of the act, referred to as Section 203(c) will expire on August 6, 1992. This section provides that prior to that date, no state or political subdivision can provide voting materials only in the English language if the director of the census determines that (1) more than five percent of the citizens of voting age of such state or political subdivisions are members of a single language minority; and (2) that the illiteracy rate of such persons as a group is higher than the national illiteracy rate. *Illiteracy,* for purposes of this section, means the failure to complete the fifth primary grade.

The act also contains provisions regarding preclearance of changes in voting laws and the possible imposition of federal examiners to ensure access to the polls by minority voters.

Immigration Laws

Under the immigration laws a person who does not have an understanding of the English language, including an ability to read, write, and speak words in ordinary usage in the English language, cannot be naturalized as a citizen. (There is an exception for persons over fifty years of age who have been living in the United States for at least twenty years after admission for permanent residence.) The statute provides that the requirements relating to English ability are met if the applicant can read or write simple words and phrases.

In 1986 Congress enacted the Immigration Reform and Control Act. Under this law, employers who knowingly hire illegal aliens or who fail to verify the identity and employment eligibility of all job applicants hired after November 6, 1986, became subject to sanctions. Because of Congressional concern that the threat of these sanctions might lead employers to discriminate against workers who look or sound foreign, Congress also incorporated a provision prohibiting discrimination against an individual in hiring or discharge based upon national origin or citizenship status. In announcing regulations interpreting this provision, the Justice Department has said that unlike Title VII of the 1964 Civil Rights Act (see Chapter 3), the immigration law prohibits intentional discrimination rather than neutral conduct with an unintended disparate impact. However, discriminatory intent under the regulations may be shown either by direct or circumstantial evidence. And in determining the standard, facially neutral policies such as English-only rules that are intended to discriminate on prohibited bases and have that effect are prohibited.

Unconscionable Contracts

The general rule in this country is that persons who are above the age of majority who are otherwise suffering from no legal infirmities have the power to enter into contracts. As a corollary to this rule, persons who enter into contracts will be bound by their bargain, even if it turns out not to have been a good bargain after all. An important exception to this rule is the situation where a court determines that contract provisions are unconscionable and therefore will not be enforced. A series of cases finds that a person's lack of English fluency may preclude equality of bargaining power. As a result, such an individual may have a defense to an attempt to enforce a contract where the language barrier precluded a knowing and intelligent meeting of the minds.

Miscellaneous State Provisions

Various state constitutional provisions and statutes also afford recognition of language rights. As indicated in the bibliography following Chapter 1, New Mexico requires pesticide labels to be printed in Spanish as well as English. It also seems to require that teachers be bilingual, although attorney general opinions have interpreted these provisions to require only that teachers be afforded an opportunity to learn Spanish. Its constitution requires the publication of laws and proposed state Constitutional amendments in English and in Spanish.

Louisiana requires the teaching of the French language and culture and history of the French populations in its public schools. The Constitution of Louisiana provides that no law shall discriminate against a person because of that person's culture. (See the discussion in Chapter 9 of the interrelation between language and culture.)

The Alaska Constitution and the Connecticut Constitution prohibit national origin discrimination. As we have seen in Chapters 3 and 5, discrimination on the basis of language has been held to constitute national origin discrimination. In addition to the Federal Voting Rights Act, several states provide for bilingual voting assistance including New Mexico, Illinois, and the District of Columbia.

Miscellaneous Federal Regulations

A number of federal regulations, in a variety of contexts, provide other protections to language minority persons. Again, the results are often somewhat inconsistent.

All required disclosures under the Federal Truth-in-Lending Act must be made in the English language, pursuant to the federal regulations applicable to this law. However, in Puerto Rico, creditors may choose to make disclosures in Spanish.

Applications for a patent must be in the English language. However, whenever an individual cannot make an oath or declaration in English, the oath or declaration attached to the application must be in a language that the individual can understand.

When a used car sale is conducted in Spanish, in a transaction covered by federal law, the window form identifying whether there are any warranties must be written in Spanish. One provision of the regulations requires display of both an English language window form and a Spanish language translation of that form. In fact, a federal regulation specifically sets out, in Spanish, the disclosure required.

Under the rules and regulations for reporting and disclosure under the Employee Retirement Income Security Act of 1974, notice in a language other than English must be given to participants under certain circumstances. Regulations require such disclosure in a non-English language for plans containing fewer than one hundred participants, in which twenty-five percent or more of all planned participants are literate only in the same non-English language. Regarding plans covering more than one hundred participants, where ten percent or more are literate only in the same non-English language or where five hundred or more participants are literate only in the same non-English language, foreign language translation must also be provided.

A regulation of the U.S. Department of Agriculture provides that labels to be affixed to packages of meat products for foreign commerce may be printed in a foreign language. A similar regulation regarding poultry also exists.

Under the statutes and regulations affecting the Coast Guard, no vessel of one hundred gross tons and upward (except those navigating rivers and the smaller inland lakes) may depart from any port of the United States unless she has on board a crew not less than seventy-five percent of which, in each department, is able to understand any order given by the officers of the vessel. Regulations allow the collector of customs to muster the crew on any vessel to require a demonstration that individual members of the crew understand the language ordinarily and customarily used by the officers in navigating and operating the ship.

This chapter contains highlights of various areas where a language right is recognized. However, it is not exhaustive. The high level of bilingualism in various parts of the country, particularly the Southwest, results in a de facto bilingualism in private as well as governmental communications. This author recalls many instances of discussions with court clerks or government officials in New Mexico, for example, in the Spanish language. Rio Arriba County, New Mexico, recently considered alternating the language used at its official county commission meetings between English and Spanish. In this author's experience, even where the official meetings of some local governing bodies in New Mexico are conducted in English, prior planning sessions often occur bilingually.

While space limitations would preclude an exhaustive listing of all state and local regulations and practices resulting in further recognition of a language right, it is important to note at this juncture that they exist. Their presence continues to fuel the language debate. For example, a woman named Emmy Shafer became an English-only convert after she allegedly could not find a clerk in the Dade County, Florida, municipal offices who could speak English to her in 1978. As a result of her experience, Ms. Shafer went on to help start the English-only movement (*Time*, December 5, 1988, p. 29).

Bibliography

Articles

Comment, *The Crown Jewel of American Liberty: The Right to Vote; What Does it Mean Under the Amended Section 2 of the Voting Rights Act*, 37 Baylor L. Rev. 1015 (1985).
Comment, *The Effects of Sections 2 and 5 of the Voting Rights Act on Minority Voting Practices*, 28 How. L.J. 589 (1985).

Selected Federal Judicial Decisions

1. *Briscoe v. Bell*, 432 U.S. 404 (1977) (re: Voting Rights).
2. *Hernandez v. Erlenbusch*, 368 F. Supp. 752 (D.C. Ore. 1973).
3. *Miranda v. Arizona*, 384 U.S. 436 (1966).
4. *Sanchez v. Lefevre*, 538 F. Supp. 1104 (S.D.N.Y. 1982) (re: Miranda warnings).
5. *Yu Cong Eng v. Trinidad*, 271 U.S. 500 (1926).

Federal Constitutional Provisions

U.S. Const. amend. XIII, XIV, XV.

Federal Statutes, Regulations

Voting Rights:
  Voting Rights Act of 1965, as amended, 42 U.S.C. § 1973, et
    seq. (1988);
  Regulations: 28 C.F.R. § 55 et seq. (1988).
Truth in Lending:
  Truth-in-Lending Act, 15 U.S.C. § 1604 (1982).
  Regulation cited: 12 C.F.R. § 226.27 (1988).
Patents:
  Regulations cited: 37 C.F.R. §§ 1.52, 1.69 (1988).
Used Car Sales:
  15 U.S.C. §§ 41, 2309 (1973, 1982).
  Regulation cited: 16 C.F.R. § 455.5 (1988).
Retirement Plans:
  Regulation cited: 29 C.F.R. § 25.20.102–2(c) (1988).
U.S. Dept. of Agriculture Labels:
  Regulations cited: 9C.F.R. § 317.7 (1988).
                      45 C.F.R. § 381.128 (1987).
Coast Guard:
  Regulation cited: 46 C.F.R. § 157.25 (1987).
Civil Rights Act (previously cited):
  42 U.S.C. §§ 1981, 1982, 1983, 1985 (1981).
Immigration:
  1. Immigration Reform and Control Act of 1986 (I.R.C.A.),
      Pub. L. No. 99–603, 100 Stat. 3359 (codified at various
      parts of the U.S. Code Annotated).
  2. 8 U.S.C. § 1423 (1988) (English language proficiency).
  3. 8 U.S.C. § 1324b (1988) nondiscrimination provision of
      I.R.C.A.).
  4. Dept. of Justice Order # 1225–87, Final Rule, Unfair Immi-
      gration-Related Employment Practices, 52 Fed. Reg. at
      37404 (10/6/87).

Other Authorities:

Statement of President Johnson during State of the Union Address, 111 Cong. Rec. 28 (daily ed. March 15, 1965), cited in 37
Baylor L. Rev. at 1020 (1985).

Miscellaneous State Provisions, Decisions

1. Frostifresh Corp. v. Reynoso, 274 N.Y.S.2d 757 (D.C. 1966), rev'd as to damages, 281 N.Y.S.2d 964 (N.Y. App. Term. 1967): (unconscionable contract resulting from language barrier).
2. N.M. Const. art. XX, § 12 (publication of laws in English and Spanish); art XII, § 8 (teachers to learn English and Spanish); art. XIX, § 1 (proposed amendments).
3. Bilingual Voting: N.M. Stat. Ann. 1–2–3 (1977); Ill. Ann. Stat. ch. 46, § 24–9 (1965); D.C. Code Ann. § 1–1309 (1981).
4. La. Const. art. I, § 3 (no cultural discrimination).
5. La. Rev. Stat. Ann. § 17–272 (West) (teaching of French language, culture, history).
6. Alaska Const. art. 1, § 3 (no national origin discrimination).
7. Conn. Const. art. 1, § 20 (no national origin discrimination).

Part Three

Formulation of an Equitable Language Rights Policy

Chapter 8

Inconsistency

Our examination of the right to language has led us through discussions of a number of contexts where our legal system recognizes such a right. By now, the reader would certainly conclude that notwithstanding the oversimplifications expressed by those who would make English the official tongue of this nation, and often repeated by courts and legislators as well, this country is not now, nor ever has been, as a matter of fact or law, monolingual. At the same time, while the preceding chapters have enabled us to view the emergence of at least the contours of a generic right to language, there are frustrating contradictions inherent in the lines of authority that produce an often elusive right for those who attempt to assert it.

The inconsistencies in our laws regarding a right to language might well be illustrated by considering the curious results which follow from applying some of the principles elicited thus far to the situation of a hypothetical Ms. Martinez.

Ms. Martinez is a United States citizen. She works part-time and also receives public assistance for her children. She is bilingual, but her primary language, and that of her school-age children, is Spanish.

Ms. Martinez is fired from her job one day because some customers complain to her boss that she spoke Spanish to a co-worker in their presence, contrary to the store's English-only rule. On the way home, she stops in a local tavern to drink a beer. The same customers are seated in the bar. When Ms. Martinez begins to tell another patron of her problems, in Spanish, the same customers object, this time to the tavern manager. The manager orders Ms. Martinez from the bar.

As it turns out, this just has not been her day. At home she learns of the status of two lawsuits filed against her several months previously by different department stores for failure to pay debts allegedly owed to them. In the first suit, Ms. Martinez had not fully understood the complaint and summons due to her language situation and had simply thrown them away, thinking they were further requests for payment. Now the store notifies her it has taken a default judgment against her. Ms. Martinez did not really understand the second complaint and summons either, but tried to answer. Now, she finds, it has been set for trial in a few days. She is very worried because she knows her English is not good enough for her to understand what will go on in the court and to enable her to explain her side of the story to the judge.

Poor Ms. Martinez's troubles are not finished for the day. Her children tell her they have been thrown out of school because their English is so bad they are flunking all of their subjects. The day's mail also brings word that the welfare assistance she receives for them has been terminated because she failed to provide information required last month by the welfare agency. Ms. Martinez understood neither the request nor the termination notice because they are written only in English.

Consider the curious results which obtain from an application of our domestic laws to Ms. Martinez's situation. She would be able to bring a lawsuit under 42 U.S.C. § 1981 against the bar owner and its customers (*Hernandez* case, Chapter 7). Yet her employment termination for exactly the same conduct would be upheld in a jurisdiction that follows the *Garcia* case (Chapter 3). (Is the right to speak Spanish more sacred in a bar than on the job?) In a jurisdiction following the *Gutierrez* case (Chapter 3), she would prevail in her employment termination case, even in the face of a state English-only statute.

Regarding her consumer problems, given our inconsistent recognition of language rights, it may turn out to have been better for her to have ignored the summons and complaint in case number one, rather than trying to answer and appear to defend herself as in case number two. After all, courts have set aside default judgments in the presence of a language barrier (see Chapter 4). However, since there is no constitutional right to an interpreter in a civil proceeding (see Chapter 4), unless the state statute or court rules provide for an interpreter, Ms. Martinez's trial in the second case may very well be a babble of voices resulting in a judgment against her even if she cannot adequately defend herself due to the language barrier.

Considering the children's situation, Ms. Martinez would find that the state could not deny her children an education based upon their language situation (see Chapter 2). It could, however, because of the language barrier, effectively deny them the food, shelter, and medical care necessary to sustain their lives while they tried to study in a jurisdiction following the *Guerrero* case (see Chapter 5).

These are admittedly dramatic, oversimplified applications. They illustrate, however, that we have not thought through whether and why we might choose to respect language differences in this country.

There are other inconsistencies as well. Suppose that Ms. Martinez is somehow able to resolve her difficulties and finds herself in a somewhat improved economic situation. She decides to purchase an automobile. Given her modest economic circumstances, she cannot afford to purchase a new vehicle, nor can she afford to pay cash for the used automobile she wishes to purchase. Under federal regulations, the seller of the used vehicle at the car lot where she chooses to do business would be required, if the sale is conducted in Spanish, to provide written notice in Spanish as to any exclusion of warranties concerning the condition of the vehicle. Because of other, inconsistent federal regulations, however, the bank would not have to include, in the loan agreement which she signs with the bank to purchase the automobile, a Spanish language disclosure of the critical terms of the loan such as the interest rate and the total of payments. There seems to be no logical reason why we would choose to force Ms. Martinez to guess at the terms of her loan, while guaranteeing that she understands the exclusion of warranties.

Other glaring inconsistencies emerge from the discussions in the preceding chapters. The U.S. Supreme Court in the *Meyer* case, for example, explicitly acknowledges that the liberty protected against infringement by the Due Process Clause includes the right "to acquire useful knowledge." In *Lau* and other cases, it cannot find a constitutional basis for bilingual education.

In the workplace, we have two potentially inconsistent lines of authority developing in the Fifth and Ninth Circuits. Irritation by monolingual English-speaking customers might justify the termination of an employee who speaks Spanish or some other foreign language to a co-worker in courts which follow the Fifth Circuit's reasoning in *Garcia v. Gloor*. Yet in the view of the Ninth Circuit, such irritation by customers and co-workers would not justify the firing.

The United States Supreme Court has never clearly stated that there is a constitutional right to an interpreter in any courtroom proceeding. Chapter 4 pointed out that the Second Circuit decision in the *Negron* case and other cases should leave little doubt that there is such a right in criminal cases. As recently as 1984, however, in a post-*Negron* decision, the Supreme Court of Wisconsin found no constitutional right to an interpreter in a criminal case. There is no constitutional basis for an interpreter in a civil or an administrative proceeding in any event, even though the relative interests at stake might be more important than in a relatively minor criminal proceeding. As a result, the extent of the right to an interpreter depends upon inconsistent statutes and regulations. The right varies, depending upon whether the litigation arises in state or federal courts, and if in the state system, upon which state one happens to be in at the time. One's interpreter, in any event, might turn out to be the attorney who is prosecuting the person with a language barrier. Or it could even be the attorney who is supposed to listen to the evidence, cross-examine, offer objections, and otherwise conduct the courtroom battle on behalf of the litigant while simultaneously furnishing an interpretation. In some cases, one's interpreter might even turn out to be the judge who reaches a verdict and imposes the sentence upon the limited English-speaking litigant.

While undocumented persons are constitutionally guaranteed an interpreter in administrative deportation proceedings (and rightfully so, in this author's opinion), it is somewhat ironic that a U.S. citizen faced with administrative proceedings with potentially severe consequences such as the termination of public assistance has no such right.

An applicant for public assistance from a non-federal entity who is unable to obtain benefits because of a language barrier may very well prevail if his or her attorney (if one has the resources to hire an attorney) invokes the statutory national origin protection but will almost certainly lose the case if the attorney bases a claim upon due process or equal protection grounds. If the federal funds flow not through a conduit, but directly from the federal government, the attorney who claims language discrimination will almost certainly lose the case in any event. Even though one line of cases holds that the equal protection and due process guarantees of the Fourteenth Amendment are basically the same protection afforded against the actions of the federal government by the Fifth Amendment's Due Process Clause, current federal court decisions have

found no constitutional violations in mere language discrimination. Somehow, litigants and courts have over-
looked the due process and equal protection bases for language protection in the *Yu Cong Eng* holding of the United
States Supreme Court (Chapter 7).

There may or may not be a right to be informed via
broadcast media in a foreign language. As a result, while a
voter arriving at the polls who suffers a language barrier
may be entitled to a bilingual ballot, he or she may not
understand the issues or the positions of the candidates
upon which he or she is voting if the public affairs programing in the local media has been presented exclusively
in English.

Seizing upon these and other inconsistencies, and cou-
pled with the recurrent hostility towards the presence of
speakers of other languages in this country, the current
proponents of English-only have arrived at a simple solution to the inconsistencies: abolish them. Make English the
official language of this nation. There is, after all, a certain
logical consistency to their position. If, in one fell swoop,
we eliminated the right to express ourselves or receive
communications in a language other than English, our
courts, administrative agencies, and legislatures would immediately be relieved of the burden of identifying, and
then paying for, programs enabling people whose English
language usage is limited to participate in governmental
programs. In the private sector, employers, co-workers,
and customers would no longer have to deal with any
frustration and resentment arising from them overhearing
an exchange of communication in a language which they
did not understand. There would be economic savings if
courts no longer had to provide interpreters or if publication of regulations and other documents did not have to
take place in a language other than English. And there
would be a resultant renewed pride in the monolingual
majority knowing that they had won a reaffirmation that
this is America, that English is the majority tongue, and
those who want to remain and be successful here should be
prepared to deal with an officially English-speaking nation.

These arguments have, in fact, won support in the recent legislative battles to make English the official language of various states.

The difficulty with this simple solution is that it is too simple. It ignores the conclusions of scholars, judges, and many lay people, as indicated throughout this book, that there are many important interests at stake in the language debate beyond mere administrative convenience and jingoistic pride in the overwhelming exclusion of foreign cultures. Another difficulty with the simple solution of the imposition of "official English" laws is that there is no empirical evidence showing that it succeeds in its objectives of decreasing the use of languages other than English or of promoting loyalty. There is, on the other hand, clear evidence and judicial findings that the presence of such statutes causes resentment and suffering among language minority peoples, with an adverse impact upon the majority as well.

The English-only approach is also overly simplistic on the issue of costs. Its thesis is that after adding up expenditures for bilingual materials, bilingualism costs too much and is a waste of societal resources. This argument has much appeal to the taxpaying public, but is too simplistic because it only considers the expenditures involved in recognition of limited language rights. Ignored are the benefits such an approach produces. It also ignores the costs involved if we fail to recognize language rights.

Expenditures alone should not determine language policy. After all, we willingly bear the expenditures required for public education and defense, and perhaps more grudgingly bear the expenditures necessary for maintaining a program of public assistance, in part because we recognize that the costs of providing such programs outweigh the larger societal costs which would result if we did not make the expenditures.

Similarly, it seems that in formulating and implementing language policies we should know and consider not only how much we will expend for bilingual education, voting, and implementation of other language rights, but also we need to know and consider the cost to society of the failure to provide adequate language assistance. Elements of this latter societal cost would include the loss resulting from children dropping out of school as a result of the frustration they feel from the rejection of their language and culture. It may be impossible to completely quantify these and all other costs resulting from our failure to afford full language rights protection. For example, we may never know the extent of the loss of productivity suffered as a result of the frustration resulting from unchallenged English-only laws in the workplace and elsewhere. We may not be able to fully quantify the lost goodwill which could result if our foreign policymakers and political leaders were able to communicate with citizens of other countries in their native tongues. We do know, though, that President Kennedy's speech containing the words in German, "I am a Berliner" produced a tremendous wave of public support for him and this country in Germany and throughout Europe in 1961. It would not require a great leap to conclude that similar benefits in our foreign relations would accrue from the ability of our leaders to make similar and more extensive pronouncements in the future.

Ignoring for the time being additional moral, legal, and other concerns (which will be discussed in the following chapters), and focusing on the simplistic costs approach of the English-only solution to language rights inconsistencies, it seems that at a minimum, further study needs to be conducted before we jump to a conclusion that it is somehow cheaper for us to impose an official language than recognize and encourage the use of other languages. For example, in addition to examining the loss resulting from educational dropouts, reduced work productivity, and lost political benefits, additional study needs to be made on the economic impact of our inability to communicate with other countries and their business people in their native languages. Will our xenophobia make us even less competitive in the world market, given the recent multinational and apparently successful multilingual cooperation which is forging the European Economic Community? Along these lines, further study needs to be done regarding why our educational institutions are apparently unable to produce people with foreign language competence who could serve to help open foreign markets. Or are we so shortsighted that we think we can prosper by only selling our products in English?

Given the current legal inconsistencies in the recognition of language rights, and given the current political appeal of the simplistic English-only movement, it would be equally oversimplistic (and probably politically unsuccessful) for proponents of the recognition of a right to language to respond to the English-only movement with mere accusations of racism. While the author has no doubt that feelings of racism play no small part in the hearts of some of the English-only proponents, it is this author's (perhaps naive) belief that the success of the English-only appeal and the confusion in the courts regarding the extent of the recognition of the right to language stem from the fact that our predominantly monolingual legal system and our predominantly monolingual academic institutions have not thought through the basic issue as to why we should recognize a right to any language other than English in this country. If this premise is correct, the first step toward striking an appropriate balance between the right of an individual to use his or her language, and legitimate societal needs, is to consider and enunciate why it is that we might choose to afford, or in some instances restrict, the right to language. That will be our next discussion.

Bibliography

(The sources relied upon in this chapter generally are cited following previous chapters. See also:

State v. Neave, 117 Wis.2d 359, 344 N.W.2d 181 (1984): no constitutional right to an interpreter in a criminal case.

Bolling v. Sharpe, 347 U.S. 497 (1954). Similarity of protection afforded against federal action by Fifth Amendment, as compared to state action under Fourteenth Amendment.

Chapter 9

Why Recognize a Right to Language?

It appears to be an unfortunate reality that many mono-lingual persons in this country feel threatened by the use of a language they do not understand, and they are hostile to the concept of legal recognition of the right to use any language other than English. Throughout the history of this nation, political and civic leaders have openly expressed such hostility and called into question the loyalty of those with differing views. (Recall, for example, the statements of Franklin, Roosevelt, and others in Chapter 1.) Scholars have expressed similar sentiments. In the early part of this century, scholarly studies allegedly proved the inferiority of foreign language immigrants. Even as recently as 1985 one scholar wrote:

> Were significant Mexican-American groups to advocate irredentist-like positions, such as open borders or *state-recognized official bilingualism*, (emphasis added) one should expect to see the growth of nativist sentiments on the part of many Americans, who would question the loyalty of Mexican-Americans. (Weiner at p. 155).

Perhaps at least part of the explanation for the inconsistent recognition of language rights in this country is that monolingual judges, legislators, political figures, scholars, and people in general carry, at least subconsciously, some of these same feelings into the decision-making process. Even those courts and legislatures which have taken a more enlightened approach to the recognition of language rights may have never completely expressed or perhaps even understood why the right to maintain a native language would be viewed by people as important, useful, beneficial, and even beautiful. As a first step to constructing the theoretical framework promised in the introduction to this book, let us examine some of the reasons why we should recognize language rights.

Interrelation of Language and Culture

In our day-to-day existence we take language for granted. If we do think about it at all, particularly if we are monolingual, we assume that "it is a vehicle equally fitted to convey any beliefs" (P. Henle, p. 1). Such a view is inconsistent with the studies of Edward Sapir. Sapir, an American linguist, maintains that:

> The relation between language and experience is often misunderstood. Language is not merely a more or less systematic inventory of the various items of experience which seem relevant to the individual, as is so often naively assumed, but is also a self-contained, creative symbolic organization, which not only refers to experience largely acquired without its help but actually defines experience for us by reason of its formal completeness and because of our unconscious projection of its implicit expectations into the field of experience. (Sapir in Henle, 1966)

Benjamin Lee Whorf, a student of Sapir, developed Sapir's claim, maintaining that language constitutes a sort of logic, a general frame of reference, and as a result, molds the thoughts of its users. He claimed that significant relationships exist between the general aspects of a language and the characteristics of the culture wherein it developed. He substantiated this thesis by comparing American Indian languages, notably Hopi, with European languages. Whorf found the differences among the European languages so insignificant in comparison to the differences between them and Hopi, that he grouped the European languages together under the title "Standard Average European" (SAE).

Henle borrowed a definition of culture as "all those historically created designs for living, explicit and implicit, rational, irrational, and non-rational, which exist at any given time as potential guides for the behavior of men." He illustrated his conclusion that world view is influenced by vocabulary and vice-versa as follows:

> The Navajo, for example, possess color terms corresponding roughly to our white, red, and yellow, but none which are equivalent to our black, gray, brown, blue, and green.
>
> They have two terms corresponding to black, one denoting the black of darkness, the other the black of such objects as coal. Our gray and brown, however, correspond to a single term in their language and likewise our blue and green. As far as vocabulary is concerned, they divide the spectrum into segments different from ours. It would seem probable that on many occasions of casual perception they would not bother to notice whether an object were brown or gray, and that they would not merely avoid discussions as to whether a shade of color in a trying light was blue or green, but they would not even make the distinction.
>
> This example must not be taken as showing that the Navajos are incapable of making color distinctions which are familiar to us. They do not suffer from a peculiar form of colorblindness any more than we do since we lack words for the two sorts of black which they distinguish. The point is rather that their vocabulary tends to let them leave other distinctions unnoticed which we habitually make.
>
> If we are right in claiming an influence of vocabulary on perception, it might be expected that vocabulary would influence other aspects of thought as well. The divisions we make in our experience depend on how we perceive and so

would be subject to the same linguistic influence as perception. Once again, one would expect the influence to run in
both directions. If, in thinking about the world, one has occasion to use certain ideas, one would expect them to be
added to the vocabulary, either directly or through meta-
phor; this is probably the primary influence. Once the term
is in the vocabulary, however, it would constitute an influence both on perception and conception. (Henle, 1966)

The causal relation between language and culture has
been documented in many other studies including writ-
ings by Burling and Blount and Sanches. Ethnolinguistics
has emerged as a field of study in the role of language in
the transmission of culture from one generation to another
(enculturation) and from one culture to another (accultura-
tion). Sociolinguistics is an even more recently emerging
field. It considers the different social roles of various languages coexisting in the same society, the development
and spread of auxiliary languages and multicultural situations or multilingual situations, the role of language in
ethnic identification, and the problems of language policy
and education.

Identifying and studying the causal relationship between language and culture is not to say which influences
the other. Scholarly criticism of the works of Sapir, Whorf,
and others lead to conflicting conclusions. As Henle notes,
"Either [language and culture] may be the causal agent,
both may be the joint effects of a common cause, or there
may be mutual causal action" (Henle at p. 5). Nonetheless,
it is clear that language and culture are inseparably interre-
lated. Perhaps the most succinct expression of this relationship is Henle's observation that "the world appears different to a person using one vocabulary than it would to a
person using another" (Henle at p. 7).

As a first step toward understanding why we should
recognize language rights, we should now have a basic
understanding as to the relationship between language
and culture. Following that line, we need to briefly consider the results which follow from the rejection by the
majority of that culture.

Social Consequences of Cultural Rejection

As we have already seen, people, particularly children who are denied the right to view the world through their language and culture, are made to feel inferior, and they react negatively. Studies involving bilingual education (see Chapter 2) and broadcasting (see Chapter 6) lead to the conclusion that the rejection of culture and the consequent poor self-image produce negative feelings that are reflected in a higher educational dropout rate, and a higher rate of acting out frustrations in the form of inappropriate behavior. The resentment may be overt and expressed in crime and other antisocial behavior. Or it may simmer at a lower level, producing alcoholism, suicide, or other self-destructive behavior. Or it may simply simmer, breeding resentment, and producing the self-fulfilling claim of disloyalty repeatedly thrown by advocates of "official English" at those who have some objections to the notion. As former Justice of the California Supreme Court Cruz Reynoso once wrote:

> High on the agenda of most Hispanic groups are the issues of bilingualism or multilingualism and biculturalism or multiculturalism. They believe that in a country as great as ours all people have a right to their own ethnicity, their own language. These rights are based on the Constitution of this country. So when there is an effort by others to take away that right there is resentment. The resentment doesn't always rise to the level of a conflict.

Rejecting the Melting Pot Ideal

Even if there is a link between language and culture, and even if people feel bad or inferior if we force them to set their language and culture aside to join the melting pot, the United States is a predominantly English-speaking country. For their own good, should not all people in this country be required to adopt the majority language and set any other aside in order to be successful here?

No one would seriously challenge the fact that English is the predominant language in this country; that social and economic pressures require one to acquire a good command of the language in order to become successful. It does not follow, though, as a matter of logic and as demonstrated by empirical research, that the native speaker of a language other than English should be officially stripped of his or her tongue in order to obtain English proficiency and obtain socioeconomic success.

Heath notes that cultural and societal forces in the United Kingdom and the United States have pushed non-native English speakers who have come to these countries as immigrants, to learn English so that they might move into the work force and achieve acceptance in the society beyond their own communities. No official national level policies in modern times mandate English. Its status as the majority tongue has been achieved without official declaration or the help of an official language academy. The primary mandate for English has come from societal forces working on an individual's desire to secure education and employment, move into English-speaking social circles, and negotiate daily interactions with the bureaucratic and commercial mainstream. Hakuta and Campbell noted that contemporary research debunks the long-held belief, rooted in work at the turn of the century on the intelligence of immigrants, that bilingualism results in mental confusion. Tienda & Neidert noted that in their studies, Spanish bilingualism (with English) does not depress socioeconomic achievement among persons who acquired a good command of English. Based on these studies and others, one could only conclude that human beings apparently have the capacity and the desire to alternatively view the world through different languages and cultures. One need not, in our free society, melt away cultural differences in order to become successful. Given the demographics as discussed in Chapter 1, some have compared our society instead to a tossed salad in which its strength lies in diversity. As the Ninth Circuit noted in the *Gutierrez* case: "The multicultural character of American society has a long and venerable history and is widely recognized as one of the United States' greatest strengths."

Practical Reasons

In addition to philosophical responses to the query "Why should we recognize a right to language?" there are some very practical reasons why this country should choose to recognize some degree of official bilingualism. First, as noted in Chapter 1, while most European immigrant groups did not pass on their language intergenerationally, Spanish is an important exception. A 1985 study estimates there were at least 13.2 million Spanish speakers in this country, representing an almost fourfold increase from the 3.3 million Spanish speakers in 1960. A number of factors identified in Chapter 1 suggest that Spanish will be maintained as an important second language in this country, notwithstanding any "official English" law.

A second very practical reason to encourage the maintenance of foreign languages is that our ignorance of them is a crippling factor in dealing with other nations. Vernon Walters, former U.S. Ambassador to the United Nations, noted in 1985 that "the failure to communicate with foreigners in their own language prevents them from understanding us as we really are. It makes it difficult for us to project our real purposes to other people." (*U.S. News and World Report*, June 15, 1985 at p. 31).

According to Hakuta and Campbell, our schools are failing to produce functional bilinguals through their foreign language programs. At the same time, we have a large population of foreign language speakers. Encouraging our bilingual citizens to maintain their linguistic diversity would guarantee that we would have a sufficiently large foreign language population to supplement our educational system's attempts at producing functional bilingual speakers. As has been noted in Chapter 1, the presence of such foreign language speakers has been of important significance in the nation's military history. It would assist us in our diplomatic relations. This in turn could only help us in our international relations, particularly with our Latin American neighbors to the south.

Third, encouraging our bilingual citizens to maintain their language skills should also produce another beneficial result in that the majority population will acquire some second language skills as well as a multicultural outlook from the bilingual population. In a 1985 survey by the Strategy Research Corporation, forty-one percent of non-Hispanics living in the Miami, Florida, area now believe that for their children to succeed, it is essential for them to read and write Spanish. Sixty percent said they enjoy socializing with Latino friends. Again, the sharing of cultures and appreciation of other languages could only result in improved internal as well as international relations.

International Obligations

The United Nations Charter, to which the United States is a party, identifies one of the purposes of the U.N. to be that of "promoting and encouraging respect for human rights and for fundamental freedoms for all without distinction as to race, sex, language, or religion."

Moreover, the Conference on Security and Co-operation in Europe, which concluded in Helsinki on August 1, 1975, resulted in a number of agreements. The United States participated in the two-year conference and signed, along with many other countries, the Final Act of the conference. That act makes reference to a number of language rights guarantees. Part 1(d)VII of the act, entitled "Respect for Human Rights and Fundamental Freedoms," provides in part:

> The participating States will respect human rights and fundamental freedoms, including the freedom of thought, con-

science, religion or belief, for all, without distinction as to race, sex, language or religion.

They will promote and encourage the effective exercise of civil, political, economic, social, cultural and other rights and freedoms all of which derive from the inherent dignity of the human person and are essential for his free and full development.

The participating States on whose territory national minorities exist will respect the right of persons belonging to such minorities to equality before the law, will afford them the full opportunity for the actual enjoyment of human rights and fundamental freedoms and will, in this manner, protect their legitimate interests in this sphere.

They confirm the right of the individual to know and act upon his rights and duties in this field.

In another section, dealing with the economic and social aspects of migrant labor we find the United States agreeing with other countries:

to regard with favour the provision of vocational training to migrant workers and, as far as possible, free instruction in the language of the host country, in the framework of their employment;

to confirm the right of migrant workers to receive, as far as possible, regular information in their own language, covering both their country of origin and the host country;

to ensure that the children of migrant workers established in the host country have access to the education usually given there, under the same conditions as the children of that country and, furthermore, to permit them to receive supplementary education in their own language, national culture, history and geography;

Another part of the agreements deals with cooperation in humanitarian and other fields. It notes that participating states, including the United States, desire to contribute to the strengthening of peace and understanding among peoples and to the spiritual enrichment of the human personality without distinction as to race, sex, language, or religion.

Each government that participated in the agreement pledged to disseminate it and make it known as widely as possible. (The actual agreement itself was drawn up in English, French, German, Italian, Russian, and Spanish.)

What About Canada?

Almost invariably, in any discussion of why we should afford recognition of language rights in this country, the English-only movement responds, "Yes, but what about Canada?" The unspoken assumption is that something dreadful has happened to our sister country to the north because it happens to recognize linguistic rights of its French-speaking minority. The comparison, which is not unlike that of apples to oranges, does not reveal anything we should fear in this country. Perhaps an admittedly brief analysis will help us understand that if anything, the Canadian language rights debate should encourage us in our attempts to define a right to language.

In 1963 the Royal Commission on Bilingualism and Biculturalism was created for the purpose of inquiring into and reporting upon the existing state of bilingualism and biculturalism in Canada, and to recommend the steps to be taken to develop the Canadian confederation on the basis of an equal partnership between the two founding nationalities (French and English). Eight years of intensive research demonstrated conclusively that the relations between the groups were far from equal. Francophiles suffered from lower socioeconomic status. Their cultural and linguistic values were largely ignored by the Anglophile majority. There was resultant friction between the groups.

The commission's conclusion was that French-Canadian discontent could be mitigated to a great extent by equality or parity in language status or practice. The relevant area for the new bilingual regime would be all of Canada (personality rather than territorial principle of language). This bilingualism, according to one scholar, Esman, aimed at convincing the French-speaking minority concentrated in Quebec that they are fairly treated and should commit their political future to Canada, rather than seeking to form a separate, French-speaking nation. (One might observe that this principle of appealing to language minority groups in their own tongue to forge national unity is not altogether dissimilar in principle from the American revolutionary experience.)

As a result, Canada enacted the Official Languages Act of 1969, which declared in paragraph 2 that "the English and French languages are the official languages of Canada." However, friction between the groups did not disappear. While more than a third of French-Canadians knew English, only five percent of the Anglophiles knew French. The act did not result in the immediate learning of the French tongue by the English majority, or an appreciation by the Anglophiles of the French culture. Instead, according to Esman, English speakers felt they, as the majority, were being asked to bear the "costs of a program they did not consider necessary, in order to buy support for Canada from an unreasonable and undeserving minority." (at p. 55). Then in 1977 the first and symbolic legislative project of the separatist "Parti Québécois" was legislation which, in effect, sought to make French the only official tongue in Quebec by, for example, denying English language education even to English-speaking immigrants unless one of their parents had been educated in the English language schools in Quebec. In measures subsequently declared unconstitutional by the Supreme Court of Canada, the new Quebec law discontinued the publication of legislative enactments and judicial decisions in English. In December 1988 the Canadian Supreme Court ruled as unconstitutional a Quebec law requiring commercial signs to be in the French language only.

Despite the continuing friction, Canada nonetheless continues to adhere to a policy of broad, official bilingualism. On July 1, 1982, its new Constitution went into effect. A new Charter of Rights and Freedoms contains, in section

16(1), the declaration that "English and French are the official languages of Canada and have equality of status and equal rights and privileges as to their use in all institutions of the Parliament and government of Canada."

There are two entirely new language guarantees, however, in this charter. First, in section 20, there is a broad right to communicate with federal institutions in either language. In section 23 there is a right for English or French language minority populations to have their children educated through the secondary level in that language. Parliament and legislature are free to "advance the equality of status or use of English or French."

However, the Supreme Court of Canada has observed that the principle of equality is a political objective, or an ideal. In three cases decided in 1986, it adopted an attitude of judicial restraint, leaving to the legislatures and political process the duty of providing for the effective advancement of the equality of official languages. As a result, the language debate continues.

Nonetheless, it is obvious that the primary political objective of national unity has been achieved. Quebec has not attempted to separate itself from the Canadian Union. The English majority has somewhat grudgingly accepted the presence of another language. Canada as a nation seems to be prospering, and has in fact recently entered into a new trade agreement with the United States. Its bilingualism has apparently not damaged its internal or external relations.

Nonetheless, there has been and will continue to be friction in Canada. One might ask, with no easy answer in sight, whether its language rights issues are a cause of, or more likely, an effect of, underlying political struggles which are not paralleled in the American experience. After all, there is no separatist threat among language minority populations in the U.S. If anything, among Hispanics, for example, there is a commitment to traditional values and patriotism. The military contribution to this nation by Hispanics is well-documented. Among Cuban and Nicaraguan populations in this country, one encounters a fervent, pro-American and anti-Communist sentiment. If there is anything to be learned from the Canadian experience, it appears to be that either wholesale rejection of language rights on the one hand, or blanket recognition of languages as official on the other, is going to perpetuate divisiveness and resentment.

Other Consequences
If We Don't Recognize the Right

Other reasons why we should recognize a right to language can be examined by considering what happens if we don't recognize a right. The path which we are now headed down appears to indicate that more states will pass English-only laws. At the same time, demographic and economic forces we have already considered suggest that the Spanish language will continue to have wider and wider use in this country. Political and economic turmoil in Latin America will continue to produce pressure on our borders and result in more native Spanish speakers arriving in this country. The virtual explosion in the broadcast media regarding the Spanish language, and an increase in advertising by American industry in Spanish, virtually guarantees that the Spanish language will continue to grow. Further, courts following the *Gutierrez* reasoning will find no difficulty in upholding federally protected rights even in the face of state English-only statutes. One might come to the conclusion then that the state statutes are harmless expressions of pride in the English language. They will not stop the increasing use of Spanish and other foreign languages. One might naively and optimistically assume that they will have no more effect than, for example, legislation requiring rain to fall upwards or the wind to quit blowing.

The reality is, however, that even though these statutes will not stop the increasing use of foreign languages, they will hurt a good many people, particularly low income people, and especially children who do not have the resources or the ability to resist the harmful effects they will produce. Recent reports in *Time* magazine and other popular media, for example, indicate that following the adoption of the California English-only constitutional provision in 1986, a great many employers began enforcing English-only rules at the workplace. Even after *Gutierrez* (see Chapter 3), a good many employers in California and elsewhere still enforce such laws. There is no practical way of knowing how many people are being denied the lawful use of their language, with the resulting frustration and tension that the unlawful enforcement of such laws and rules creates. There is no practical way of knowing how many people have been terminated from their employment because of these rules without the resources or even the knowledge to bring a lawsuit challenging them. Litigation is, after all, a lengthy, protracted, and expensive process. Even where people know that they have the rights protected by *Gutierrez*, they simply may not have the ability or the will to resist. There is no way of knowing, as a practical matter, how many other instances of language discrimination will go unnoticed or unresolved.

Well-meaning people may seriously be misled to believe that the existence of a state English-only statute not only permits, but even requires the imposition of English-only rules at work, in administrative agencies, and in other settings. Some not-so-well-intentioned people may use these statutes as a pretext for further discrimination. The legal system is, after all, extremely complex and incomprehensible to most lay people. Its intricacies are not often understood even by those learned in the law. Recall, for example, that the enforcers of the unlawful English-only law in the *Gutierrez* case were municipal judges.

The continuing press for state legislation and the existence of state statutes will only produce additional instances of language discrimination, hostility, and disorder in our society. As recently as December 5, 1988, for example, *Time* magazine reported that the city council in Monterey Park (a suburb of Los Angeles) ousted the trustees of the library for buying foreign language books and magazines. (Nearly three-quarters of the books in the Library of Congress are in languages other than English, reflecting the view of the Librarian of Congress that the multilingual collection "expresses the special character" of our multilingual nation. Boorstin, pp. 52, 53). At a Los Angeles hospital, the head nurse forbade workers to speak anything but English and urged employees to report anyone overheard using another language. The manager of an insurance company in Los Angeles ordered Chinese-American staffers to speak only English unless they were dealing with a Chinese-speaking customer. None of these actions is made lawful, nor required by, an English-only provision in the state constitution. They are hurting people and causing resentment.

The existence of English-only laws also leads to the mistaken notion that their existence will remove other federally protected rights. Media in Texas reported in December 1988 that a new "official English" movement has sprung up as a result of the efforts of an individual who, in 1976, went to his Democratic precinct to vote and saw Spanish and English on the ballot for the first time: "I couldn't see why our country was engaged in pandering—which is what it seemed to me—to one ethnic group when there are many other ethnic groups in this country." Such is the reason cited for this new English-only movement in Texas. Its founder announced the formation of the American Ethnic Coalition, which he says will not rest until his native state of Texas recognizes English as its official language. The founder of this organization is either misinformed as to the law or is engaged in deliberate spreading of misinformation. Recall that the right to a bilingual ballot in some areas is protected under the Federal Voting Rights Act of 1965 (see Chapter 7). Under the Supremacy Clause of the United States Constitution, federal statutes would prevail over state statutes that conflicted with them. Thus, even if Texas were to make English the official language of the state, federally protected voting rights would not be affected.

However, many people will undoubtedly join in the movement under the mistaken belief that the passage of the state statute will abolish bilingual ballots. When and if they succeed in making English the official language of Texas, they will learn to their dismay that the federal law is not affected. In the meantime, their campaign will have provoked a good deal of resentment among Spanish-speaking citizens. It may have intimidated voters who need and deserve language assistance. And upon the realization that the state statute is inadequate to eradicate bilingual ballots, English-only proponents will undoubtedly be persuaded that the next step is to move toward adopting the federal constitutional amendment making English the official language. (It is the opinion of this author that the attempts to create state English-only statutes are a strategic first move in attempting to obtain a federal amendment. In the constitutional ratification process, supporters would then be able to point to state statutes in urging voters to ratify the federal amendment, arguing that the federal constitutional amendment would not be that big of a change, because after all, the state already has an "official English" statute in effect.)

In this vein, consider what would happen if we choose not to recognize language rights and allow the enactment of a constitutional amendment on the federal level making English the official language. In its form as advocated by former Senator Hayakawa, it would immediately return our criminal courts to a babble of voices for many people. It would disenfranchise many of our voters. It would impose second-class status and feelings of inferiority upon many of our children. It would signal the other nations of the world that we are not yet ready to join them in an attempt to appreciate any world view other than our own. Even the latest proposal by Representative Shumway, which nominally provides for some educational instruction in a language other than English, and allows translators in courts and in other circumstances, would be a radical, damaging, and unnecessary alteration of this nation's decision not to officially impose any language upon its populace. It would abolish, for example, the bilingual access to the ballot guaranteed by the Voting Rights Act. The right to exercise this franchise has been described by former President Reagan as the "crown jewel" in American democracy. Representative Shumway would snatch that, and other jewels, from American citizens. His statement before the House Committee on the Judiciary Subcommittee on Civil and Constitutional Rights of May 11, 1988, characterizes opponents to his bill as "having no substantive arguments to present," and indicate that they rely "upon ridiculous, unfounded, highly emotional accusations." It is clear from the text of the proposed amendment and the tenor of the arguments advanced for it, that anyone who dares oppose it will be labeled in the same fashion, with the hints of disloyalty that accompany proponents' remarks directed at opponents of these proposals.

The proponents of a federal constitutional "official English" amendment are either ignorant of, or deliberately fail to mention, the language rights that have developed in the number of contexts we have already examined. Rather, in their arguments, they focus upon the most visible and controversial areas of bilingualism (including voting rights, bilingual education and often the work place), with no mention of the historical, legal, sociological, political, and economic concerns which have led this nation to its official linguistic neutrality.

The Moral Issues

Given that there are already a wide array of protected language rights, and given that it is unlikely that these rights will be abolished, there are serious moral questions raised by the attempts to promote and enact "official English" statutes. Is it fair to impose hardships upon language minority people, particularly children, in order to discourage those people from the exercise of federally protected rights? Is it fair to create an atmosphere of hostility toward languages other than English, which results in hostility against the speakers of those languages?

The recent increase in immigration has apparently inflamed nativist resentments, as has occurred in the past (see Chapter 1). In an attempt to limit immigration, there has been an unfortunate tendency in this country to make life as difficult as possible for the new arrivals to discourage them and future immigrants from arriving or staying here. For example, a legislative scheme was created in Texas in the early 1980s that withheld from local school districts any state funds for the education of children not legally admitted into the United States, and authorizing local school districts to deny these children enrollment. The implicit purpose was to punish children of the undocumented to discourage those parents from staying here and to discourage other parents and potential parents from either illegally bringing their children to this country or from giving birth here to United States citizen children. When the statute was challenged, the United States Supreme Court in 1982 concluded that the scheme was inconsistent with the Equal Protection Clause of the Fourteenth Amendment. It noted that even if the state found it expedient to control the conduct of adults by acting against their children, legislation directing the onus of a parent's misconduct against his or her children does not comport with fundamental conceptions of justice: "Visiting condemnation on the head of an infant is illogical and unjust."

In another case this author brought suit in federal court to get welfare officials in the state of Kansas to provide public assistance to the citizen children of undocumented parents. Welfare officials took the position that providing public assistance to those citizens would only encourage further illegal immigration. Their position was clearly unlawful, and the benefits were eventually provided by settlement. These and many other cases indicate that there is an unfortunate recent willingness in this country to act even against children, even against citizen children, in order to discourage immigration and to make life harder for those who do immigrate.

The language issue is similar. We are imposing a hardship upon people, even upon our own citizens, even upon our own children, even in the face of federally protected rights, because of a xenophobic fear of the presence of other languages and cultures. Much of the heat of the current debate, after all, is generated in the context of bilingual education for citizen children. For these children and their parents, the English-only initiatives shout, "You are here but we would like to make it difficult for you" (remarks of Coleen O'Connor, *Time*, December 5, 1988).

For many of the opponents of language rights, the "official English" movement is a socially acceptable way of tapping into nativist fears of being outnumbered by immigrants and fear of anyone different. The increasing Hispanic presence is viewed as a threat. As the cofounder of U.S. English explains in a 1986 memo in which he expressed concern that low birth rates among whites and high birthrates among Hispanics would "endanger" American society, Dr. Tanton noted: "Perhaps this is the first instance in which those with their pants up are going to get caught by those with their pants down." In these circumstances it becomes clear that the failure to explicitly recognize a right to language encourages a backlash against immigrants. It is a backlash that is expressed in legislative and other attempts to make life as difficult and unbearable here as possible for the new arrivals, and reverberates not only against immigrants but upon natives as well.

Other questions are raised. We know that monolingual persons often feel resentment and suspicion toward persons speaking another language. But why should that resentment justify stripping others of their foreign language ability? Why should we, as a free and democratic society, cater to the prejudices of some under the guise of promoting national unity, when we know that English-only rules

create an atmosphere of inferiority, isolation, and intimidation, and increase rather than decrease racial tension? (see
Gutierrez.) When there is evidence that our people have the
ability and the desire to view the world through different
languages and cultures why should we attempt to shut off
the view? Given the important historical, economic, political, artistic, academic, and military contributions to this
society of language minorities, do we seriously have any
grounds to believe that the presence of their languages and
cultures is promoting disloyalty or otherwise causing a
disadvantage to our nation's sovereignty?

There are other moral and human rights issues to consider in attempting to answer the question as to why we
should recognize a right to language in this country. They
might be illustrated by asking the reader to consider several scenarios, which could occur in the absence of a recognition of language rights.

Try to remember what it felt like to be five or six years
old, going to school for the first time. Now imagine that
your name is Teresita. Your parents are lawful immigrants
to the United States. You were born in this country. Your
parents and you speak some English, and you are used to
hearing that language on T.V. Spanish is still the primary
language spoken in your home, in large part because your
grandparents who live with you do not speak English. You
are proud of your hard-working, religious family. Yet you
feel some anxiety as your mother puts some tortillas and
lunch meat into a sack for your lunch, walks you to school,
and hugs you goodbye.

In the classroom, the teacher speaks English in a rapid
fashion. You do not completely understand her. She is
calling roll, and all the other kids have Anglo names. When
she gets to your name she stumbles over it, and she and the
children laugh. Your stomach begins to hurt. "Well, never
mind, kids. This name is too hard for me to pronounce."
Looking at you she says, "From now on your name in this
class will be 'Terry.'" She smiles and you don't feel well.

You struggle through the morning's classes. You have

always done well with the counting and reading and saying the prayers your mother has taught you. But this is different. When the teacher asks the class what is one plus one your hand is the first to shoot up. "Dos," you answer quickly, when the teacher points to you. The other children and the teacher laugh again. At lunchtime you pull the tortillas from your sack. The other children are looking at you. You can't eat.

That afternoon your mother waits for you on the school ground. "How was school?" she asks you in Spanish. You don't want to disappoint her because you know how important she and your father feel it is for you to do well in school. "It was fine. The teacher gave me a new name. She said my name is now 'Terry.'" Your mother looks at you with an expression you don't understand. Tears fill her eyes, she bends down, looks in your eyes, then hugs you. The rest of the kids are looking at you again.

Now imagine that you are a bilingual construction worker. You are proud of the work performed by you and your crew. In fact most of the workers in your unit are people you grew up with in the barrio in which you were raised. You socialize with them—Hispanics and Anglos alike—after work, and are generally quite pleased with your job. One day a new foreman is hired. He does not speak Spanish, and orders you and the other workers to quit communicating with each other in what he calls Mexican. When you try to object he orders you to shut up and speak American. You need the job so you shut up, but you can't help think of your high school civics teacher telling you that the slaves couldn't speak to each other in their native tongues either, because the slave owners feared that would lead to rebellion. And you can't help but think of the aging photos of your dad and some of his buddies who were decorated for their service in Bataan. Your foreman has no military service record.

Finally, imagine that you are elderly and infirm. One morning upon arising, you feel severe chest pains and numbness in your arms. You reach the phone, and call for your doctor, but the office is not yet open. You dial the official emergency number, and in your best English, ask for help. The dispatcher cannot understand you completely because of your accent, and grows impatient. "Please," you repeat. "Help." You give your address again. As you begin to lose consciousness, you wonder whether an ambulance will be sent, and if so, whether it will reach you in time.

These examples are admittedly emotional appeals. Law and language issues are clearly emotional as well as legal issues. (One of the ironies of this current debate is that the proponents of "official English" who resort to claims of disloyalty and preserving the Anglo race against the so-called disease of other languages and cultures will then claim that the responses these accusations provoke are merely emotional). Nonetheless, it is the author's hope that these examples help illustrate some of the moral and human rights issues involved in a consideration of why we should recognize a right to language in this country.

Bibliography

Books

D. Boorstin, *The Republic of Letters* (J. Cole, ed. 1989).
P. Henle, *Language, Thought and Culture* (1966).
Blount & Sanches, *Sociocultural Dimensions of Language Change* (1977).
K. Hakuta, *Mirror of Language* (1986).

Articles

1. Bastarche, Language Legislation: The Canadian Experience, handout at "Linguistic Rights and Minority Groups: A Canadian-American Comparison," Canadian-Amer

ican Interests Section, Association of American Law Schools Annual Meeting, New Orleans (Jan. 6, 1989) (copy on file with this author).

2. Esman, "The Politics of Official Bilingualism in Canada," in *Language Policy and National Unity* (Beer and Jacob, eds. 1985).

3. Hakuta and Campbell, *The Future of Bilingual Education* C.O.S.S.A., Washington Update, Consortium of Social Science Associations (Mar. 22, 1985).

4. Heath, *A National Language Academy: Debate in the New Nation*, 11 Int'l. J. Soc. Language 9–44 (1976).

5. Heath, Language Policies: "Patterns of Retention and Maintenance," in *Mexican-Americans In Comparative Perspective* (W. Connor ed. 1985).

6. Kluckhohn & Kelly, "The Concept of Culture," in *The Science of Man In the World Crises* (1945).

7. Landry, Outline of Topics, handout at "Linguistic Rights and Minority Groups: A Canadian-American Comparison," Canadian-American Interests Section, Association of American Law Schools Annual Meeting, New Orleans (Jan. 6, 1989) (copy on file with this author).

8. Piatt, *Born as Second-Class Citizens In the U.S.A.: Children of Undocumented Parents*, 63 Notre Dame L. Rev. 35 (1988).

9. Piatt, *Toward Domestic Recognition of a Human Right to Language*, 23 Hous. L. Rev. 885 (1986).

10. Reynoso, "Community Dispute Resolution: Hispanic Concerns," in *The Elements of Good Practice in Dispute Resolution*, p. 215 (1985).

11. Tienda & Neidert, "Language, Education, and the Socioeconomic Achievement of Hispanic Origin Men," in *The Mexican-American Experience* (1974).

12. Weiner, "Transborder Peoples," in *Mexican-Americans In Comparative Perspective* (W. Connor, ed. 1985).

Federal Sources

1. U.S. Const. art. VI (Supremacy Clause).
2. *Plyler v. Doe*, 457 U.S. 202 (1982).

Canadian Legal Sources

1. Official Languages Act of 1969.
2. Bill 101 of August 1977 (Quebec).
3. Charter of Rights and Freedoms.
4. *Societe de Acadiens du Nouveau-Brunswick v. Association of Parents for Fairness in Education* (1986), 1 S.C.R. 549.

Other Sources

United Nations Charter, 59 Stat. 1033, 1037 (1945).

Conference on Security and Cooperation in Europe, Final Act, August 1, 1975, 14 I.L.M. 1293.

Taped remarks of participants, "Linguistic Rights and Minority Groups: A Canadian-American Comparison," Canadian-American Interests Section, Association of American Law Schools Annual Meeting, New Orleans (Jan. 6, 1989) (copy on file with this author).

Chapter 10

Accommodation

An important result of the current debate is that it requires us to think through something we daily take for granted: the use of language. Further thought and study seem appropriate. Indeed, the frustration of writing this book is that any one of the chapters could and should be expanded into book length in order to more effectively analyze the issues involved. This work, then, does not pretend to be the last word on law and language policy. Rather, it should serve as the impetus for further study and analysis.

In that vein, let me suggest an approach toward accommodation of the various interests at stake. Assuming that we wish to recognize some legal protection and recognition of a right to language, the problem is to develop an analytical framework that fairly takes into account legitimate societal needs, and the rights of the individual who speaks a language other than English.

The first step in developing this framework is to identify the real interests which we seek to protect when we recognize language rights. These interests appear to be the individual's rights to: (1) view the world through his or her own language and culture, and (2) not be shut off from the exercise of some fundamental legal right or the satisfaction of some basic human need because of a language barrier.

At the present time, courts are only able to inconsistently protect these interests because the theoretical concepts upon which their decisions rest are analytically unsound and perpetuate confusion. For example, this writer would eventually abandon the concept which forces protection of language rights into the national origin pigeonhole (see Chapters 2, 3, and 5). Many of those individuals whose language rights we would protect are native-born United States citizens. Using a national origin fiction is thus analytically unsound, and may perpetuate the fear of some monolingual persons that the use of a language other than English is foreign.

This writer would also urge abandoning the concept, particularly in the bilingual education context, that protection of the recognition of a right to use another language should only exist until English is acquired. This transitional approach is found in the education context. It also appears in work-rule cases such as *Garcia v. Gloor,* which find no language protection once English is acquired, under the theory of mutability. The theory is that once a person who speaks a foreign language acquires English language ability, the language which that person speaks is a matter of choice. Society has the right to limit the choice to English. There are then only shallow, if any attempts, to justify limiting the individual's choice once courts identify language as mutable. (In *Garcia,* you will recall, the court made no attempt to critically evaluate whether there were any valid business reasons for the English-only rule. It deferred largely to the apparent irritation of monolingual customers who resented the bilingual worker's choice of language in brief communication with a co-worker.)

One problem with this mutability analysis is that it fails to take into account the individual's interest in viewing the world through his or her culture (see Chapter 9). It also fails to inquire whether there are less restrictive measures available to satisfy the majority's concerns, rather than resorting to blanket denials of the right to another world view. It is inconsistent with the analogous treatment of a

right to a religious identity. Even though language is mutable, so too is the exercise of religious beliefs. No one would
seriously argue that the choice of a world view through the
eyes of a particular religion should be subject to govern-
ment-enforced change. The United Nations charter, as
noted (Chapter 9), identifies one of the purposes of the
United Nations to be that of "promoting and encouraging
respect for human rights and for fundamental freedoms
for all without distinction as to race, sex, language, or
religion." There is national and international legal authority for the notion that language and religion, though mutable, are matters of individual choice and not government
fiat.

This writer would also abandon the notion that English
or any other language be made the official language of the
United States. As previously noted, such a solution would
ignore demographic and economic realities. It would provoke racial tension rather than provide unification. It
would ultimately lead to returning our courts to babbles of
voices, would disenfranchise many voters, impose second-
class status and feelings of inferiority upon many of our
children, be inconsistent with the long-established notion
of language liberty, and not cause any language to disappear. It would unnecessarily impose hardship on many
people, particularly those least able to protect themselves.
There is even some serious thought that a federal constitutional amendment proclaiming English to be the official
language, and removing language minority people from
effective participation in the democratic process, would be
unconstitutional. (Are there some freedoms so inherently
fundamental to our American experiment with democracy
that they could not be removed even with an amendment
to the Constitution?)

The existing patchwork protection of language rights
should be replaced with an analysis that can be summarized as follows:

1. Where, because of a language barrier, an individual is
denied the exercise of a fundamental legal right or denied

access to a basic human need, society would recognize limited official bilingualism in order to allow access to the right or the need;

2. Where circumstances require communications in one standard language understood by the majority, for the immediate safety of persons or property, society would recognize limited official monolingualism;

3.   In the vast majority of other communications, individuals would be free to utilize any language of choice, and society would provide a remedy for the infringement of that choice.

Having sketched the outline, let us turn to filling it in.

Limited Official Bilingualism

Courts have demonstrated proficiency in identifying Bill of Rights guarantees so fundamental to the American scheme of justice so as to apply to the states via the Due Process Clause of the Fourteenth Amendment (see Chapter 2). They have also been able to identify, among others, the right to travel, the right to vote, and the right to properly defend oneself in criminal proceedings as fundamental interests for equal protection purposes. Where the exercise of such rights is prohibited by one's poverty, courts have determined that the right or interest is so fundamental that society should provide assistance so that the right can be exercised. For example, an indigent now has a right to state provided counsel in criminal matters, and, absent a knowing waiver, may not be imprisoned for any offense unless represented by counsel. Indigents are also entitled to state-provided appellate counsel and trial transcripts for use on appeal where a state statute gives a right to a person convicted of a crime to lodge such an appeal. Similarly, courts and legislatures have implicitly recognized that there are some fundamental rights, such as the right to confront witnesses in a criminal trial (see Chapter 4) or the right to vote (see Chapter 7) which cannot effectively be exercised by a person who does not understand the procedure due to a language barrier. In such cases, society provides interpreters or bilingual materials to allow the exercise of the right.

Courts and legislatures should continue the process of identifying the fundamental legal rights which should not be foreclosed to persons with a language barrier. Where such a right is identified, society should provide bilingual assistance where the right would otherwise be foreclosed to persons with limited English proficiency. Courts and legislatures should be explicit in identifying that the reason for the statute or the case holding is to protect, as a matter of due process and equal protection, the exercise of the fundamental right which is otherwise foreclosed. Courts and legislatures should make such determinations after explicit pronouncements that the right is so fundamental that it should not be foreclosed to persons with a language barrier just as it will not be foreclosed to persons with an economic barrier.

One area where the right should be extended immediately is in the civil courts and before administrative bodies. The relative financial interests at stake (for example, tenant eviction proceedings or hearings to terminate public assistance) may be greater than in relatively minor criminal proceedings. We choose not to allow our criminal courts to be a babble of voices (see Chapter 4). We have the right to maintain business records in an understandable language (see Chapter 7). Why should not litigants in civil and administrative proceedings be afforded more than the facade of justice that may now exist for those not completely proficient in English?

There are other needs which, although not categorized by our system of jurisprudence as fundamental rights would nonetheless be recognized by us as basic to our survival and advancement as a species. Among these would be the need for food and shelter and a basic education. (Maslow identified a hierarchy of needs ranging from the lowest and most urgent such as food, shelter, and clothes to higher, nonmaterial needs which are also basic, including respect, esteem, dignity, and freedom for the fullest development of one's talents.) Where a human being in our society would otherwise be entitled to have at least the basic material needs met by means of public assistance or public education, society should allow the person with a language barrier access to them. In the case of public assistance, we should provide interpreters to assist with the application process and through any administrative hearings that are otherwise available. In the case of public education, given the profound negative impact upon children whose language and culture are rejected by monolingual institutions (see Chapters 2 and 6), we should recognize a right to bilingual education. Again, courts and legislatures should be quite explicit in identifying and announcing the theoretical bases for the recognition.

Acknowledging a right to bilingual education would undoubtedly be controversial. We noted in Chapter 2 the bitter attacks made upon the concept. Yet the self-image and future success of our children is profoundly affected by the majority's acceptance or nonacceptance of their language and culture. We could be utilizing their language skills and thought processes to foster intellectual development while simultaneously assisting them in obtaining English language proficiency. It should not be necessary for them to sacrifice their rich native language, culture, and self-esteem in order to participate in the educational system and in society. We cannot afford, at this late date, to return to punishing our children for viewing the world through their language and culture.

Implementing this move to limited official bilingualism would require an overhaul of legislative enactments and judicial precedents. Undoubtedly it would be costly. The same things can be said, however, of the recognition of a right to state provided transcripts or attorneys for indigents facing the criminal process. In those cases, courts identified the rights as fundamental, knowing that additional economic burdens would be placed upon the state. The duty to alleviate the deprivation of rights that cannot be exercised because of a language barrier has already, however, been held to be clear and compelling, notwithstanding that there may be practical problems to overcome in providing complete and effective relief.

We have already made commitment of societal resources in the areas of bilingual education, voting rights, and court interpreters. The wheel need not be reinvented. The *Carmona* case, for example (see Chapter 5), based its conclusion that California need not provide interpreters in the administration of its unemployment insurance program in part on a finding that provision of interpreters in the Spanish language would impose additional burdens on California's resources. Since *Carmona*, the United States court system has adopted and implemented guidelines for the certification and use of interpreters (see Chapter 2).

Interpreters certified in federal courts could be utilized in administrative proceedings without the cost of training and certification. The increasing bilingual ability of Spanish speakers in this country could be put to use in producing forms and providing informal translations. A Wilson library bulletin in January 1986 indicates that libraries across the country now have access to information regarding educational materials and languages other than English. Moreover, before concluding that the cost of provision of interpreters and language assistance should prohibit the furnishing of such materials, society should consider not only the cost of such bilingual implementation, but the societal cost of dropouts among children who feel frustrated as a result of the rejection of language and culture (see Chapter 8).

This call for explicit recognition of even limited official bilingualism will undoubtedly provoke cries that such factionalism would produce the multicultural competition and tension supposedly exhibited in countries where more than one language is recognized. It would inevitably lead to the repeated allegation by proponents of English-only that the implicit recognition of more than one language in this country would result in the same factionalism as Canada or other countries. This author urges further study on this point. Initially, however, it appears that the tension over multilingualism in Canada is in part the result of political struggles between competing English- and French-speaking populations, and not necessarily the sole cause of it. Despite the xenophobic fears of many of the English-only proponents, there is no indication of disloyalty to the United States among Spanish-speaking population groups. Mexican-Americans take pride in commitment to traditional values. Hispanics point with pride to the military contributions to this nation from the time of the revolution to the present. Hispanics count thirty-seven Medal of Honor winners, a higher percentage than English-speaking Anglo-Americans. Cuban-Americans who fled the Castro government, and new arrivals from Nicaragua and other Latin American governments, exhibit a high degree of identification with American ideals and in fact, constitute one of the most outspoken anti-Communist groups in this country. News programing and public affairs presentations on Univision (a Spanish language television network) would have to be identified as consistently more conservative than any of the major English-speaking networks in this country.

The fact that some other countries recognize official languages and thereby officially exclude others should not justify restricting language rights in this nation. After all, up to this point at least, we have viewed ourselves as the beacon of human liberties, and the standard against which other countries' human rights policies should be measured. We should not now begin to adopt a least common denominator approach, limiting human rights in this nation merely because we can point to other countries that do the same.

Limited Official Monolingualism

There are circumstances where communication in English should be required. Allowing airplane pilots, for example, to communicate with each other and the ground in any language of choice could be inherently dangerous to person and property. There are other communications, such as traffic signs or emergency communications, that society should require to be made in the majority language to protect persons and property from the immediate risk of harm. Similarly, although not on the emergency level, employers should be free to require their employees to communicate with potential customers in the language of the customer's choice to facilitate commerce and protect the employer's property interest in the business. In recognizing limited official monolingualism, society should place the burden on the proponent of the enforced monolingualism to demonstrate that the danger to person or property outweighs the individual right to expression before opposing the use of the language. Irritation by monolingual customers or other third parties would be insufficient justification for the imposition of the majority language. After all, in other contexts, irritation has been held not to justify what otherwise would be unlawful discrimination. Thus, in an important employment case, a customer preference for female stewardesses was held insufficient justification for refusal by an airline to hire men for the same jobs. We also have the *Hernandez* (see Chapter 7) observation that catering to prejudice out of fear of provoking greater prejudice only perpetuates racism.

Language of Choice in Other Circumstances

In the vast range of remaining communications, government should adhere to its tradition of adopting no official language nor denying personal liberties in language selection. Courts would provide a remedy for private interference with language use, consistent with the *Hernandez* case (see Chapter 7). Our courts, legislatures, and administrative bodies should begin to make explicit, as did the court in *Gutierrez*, that the multicultural character of Ameri-

can society has a long and venerable history and is widely
recognized as one of the United States greatest strengths.
They should publicly and repeatedly confirm that even
though an individual may learn English and become assimilated into American society, his or her primary language
remains an important link to ethnic culture and identity,
with the language conveying not only concepts but serving
as an affirmation of that primary culture. They should recognize as did the court in *Gutierrez* that English-only rules
create an atmosphere of inferiority, isolation, and intimidation, serve as pretexts for discrimination, and increase
rather than decrease racial hostility. They should acknowledge that existing racial fears or prejudices and their effects
cannot justify the imposition of burdens upon a language
group. By so doing, they will reaffirm the conclusion of the
Founding Fathers of this nation that loyalty to our democracy would best be promoted among differing cultural
groups by permitting the use of their language and even
appealing to them in their native language rather than by
the totalitarian imposition of a government-sanctioned language.

Bibliography

Books

Maslow, *Toward a Psychology of Being* (1962).

Articles

Piatt, *Born as Second-Class Citizens in the U.S.A.: Children of Un-
documented Parents*, 63 Notre Dame L. Rev. 35 (1988).
Piatt, *Toward Domestic Recognition of a Human Right to Language*, 23
Hous. L. Rev. 885 (1986).
Valentine, *Minority Language Selection: Helping Ourselves to Help
Others*, Wilson Library Bulletin (Jan. 1986).

Selected Federal Judicial Decisions

1. *Argersinger v. Hamlin*, 407 U.S. 25 (1963) (indigent has right to counsel and absent waiver, may not be imprisoned unless represented by counsel).
2. *Benton v. Maryland*, 395 U.S. 784 (1969) ("fundamental" rights).
3. *Diaz v. Pan Am World Airways, Inc.*, 442 F.2d 385 (5th Cir. 1971) (customer preference for female stewardesses insufficient justification for refusal to hire men).
4. *Douglas v. California*, 372 U.S. 353 (1963) (indigents have right to state-appointed counsel).
5. *Griffin v. Illinois*, 351 U.S. 12 (1956) (indigents entitled to state-provided trial transcript).
6. *Harper v. Virginia Bd. of Elections*, 383 U.S. 663 (1966) (right to vote is fundamental).
7. *Shapiro v. Thompson*, 394 U.S. 618 (1969) (right to travel is a fundamental right).

Table of Cases

191

Case	Page(s) where case cited or principle applied
2 Fair Empl. Prac. Cas (BNA) No. YAU 9N-1048 at 78 (June 30, 1969)	61
Federal Radio Commission v. Nelson Bros. Bond & Mortgage Co., 289 U.S. 266 (1933)	114
Fragante v. City and County of Honolulu, ___ F.2d ___, 57 U.S.L.W. 2557 (4/4/89) (9th Cir. 1989)	62
Frontera v. Sindell, 522 F.2d 1215 (6th Cir. 1975)	101, 102
Frostifresh Corp. v. Reynoso, 274 N.Y.S.2d 757 (D.C. 1966), rev'd as to damages, 281 N.Y.S. 2d 964 (N.Y. App. Term. 1967)	136
Garcia v. Gloor, 618 F.2d 264 (5th Cir. 1980)	67, 69, 72, 147, 148, 180
Goldberg v. Kelly, 397 U.S. 254 (1970)	100
Griffin v. Illinois, 351 U.S. 12 (1956)	182
Guerrero v. Carlson, 9 Cal.3d 808, 512 P.2d 833, 109 Cal Rptr. 201 (1973)	98, 99, 103, 105, 108, 147
Guerrero v. Harris, 461 F.Supp. 583 (S.D.N.Y. 1978)	83
Gutierrez v. Municipal Court, 838 F.2d 1031 (9th Cir. 1988), vacated as moot, 57 U.S.L.W. 3687 (4/18/89)	26, 28, 59, 69, 71, 73, 147, 160, 167, 168, 173, 187, 188
Harper v. Virginia Bd. of Elections, 383 U.S. 663 (1966)	182
Hernandez v. Erlenbusch, 368 F. Supp. 752 (D.C. Ore. 1973)	130, 146, 187
Ho Ah Kow v. Nunan, 5 Sawyer 552 (C.C.D. Cal. 1879)	29
In Re Great Lakes Television, Inc., 255 F.C.C. 470 (1958)	116
In Re La Fiesta Broadcasting Co., 6 F.C.C. 2d 65 (1966)	116
Jara v. Municipal Court, 21 Cal. 3d 181, 578 P.2d 94, 145 Cal. Rptr. 847 (1978)	81
Jones v. United Gas Imp. Corp., 68 F.R.D. 1 (E.D. Pa. 1975)	61
Jurado v. Eleven-Fifty Corp., 813 F.2d 1406 (9th Cir. 1988)	70
Lau v. Nichols, 414 U.S. 563 (1974)	43, 45, 46, 47, 105

Case	Page(s) where case cited or principle applied
Martin Luther King Jr. Elem. School Children v. Ann Arbor School Dist. Bd., 473 F. Supp. 1371 (E.D. Mich. 1979)	53, 54
Mendoza v. Lavine, 412 F. Supp. 1105 (S.D.N.Y. 1976), 91 F.R.D. 91 (1981), 560 F.Supp. 284 (1983)	104, 109, 110
Meyer v. Nebraska, 262 U.S. 390 (1923)	29, 38, 39, 40, 42, 52, 99, 129
Miranda v. Arizona, 384 U.S. 436 (1966)	132
National Broadcasting Co. v. United States, 319 U.S. 190 (1943)	115
New Mexico Broadcasting Co., 87 F.C.C. 2d 213 (1981)	130, 131
Pabon v. Levine, 70 F.R.D. 674 (S.D.N.Y. 1976)	107
Patterson v. McClean Credit Union, 109 S.Ct. 2363 (1989)	76
People v. Estrada, 176 Cal. App. 3d 410, 221 Cal. Rptr. 922 (1986)	88
Perovich v. United States, 205 U.S. 86 (1907)	80
Plyler v. Doe, 457 U.S. 202 (1982)	53
Red Lion Broadcasting Co. v. F.C.C., 395 U.S. 367 (1969)	121, 122
Retana v. Apartment Operators Local 14, 453 F.2d 1018 (9th Cir. 1972)	75
Rosa v. Weinberger, 381 F.Supp. 377 (E.D.N.Y. 1974)	107
San Antonio Indep. School Dist. v. Rodriquez, 411 U.S. 1 (1973)	53
Sanchez v. LeFevre, 538 F.Supp. 1104 (S.D.N.Y. 1982)	132
Saucedo v. Brothers Well Serv., Inc., 464 F.Supp. 919 (S.D. Tex. 1979)	66, 67
Seltzer v. Foley, 502 F.Supp. 600 (S.D.N.Y. 1980)	84
Serna v. Portales Mun. Schools, 351 F. Supp. 1279 (D.N.M. 1972), *aff'd*, 499 F.2d 1147 (10th Cir. 1974)	44, 45, 47, 105
Shapiro v. Thompson, 394 U.S. 618 (1969)	182
Smith v. Turner, 48 U.S. 283 (1849)	14
Soberal-Perez v. Heckler, 466 U.S. 929 (1984)	102, 110

Index